Creating a Useful Science of Education

Creating a Useful Science of Education

Society's Most Important and Challenging Task

R. Barker Bausell

ROWMAN & LITTLEFIELD
Lanham • Boulder • New York • London

Published by Rowman & Littlefield
A wholly owned subsidiary of The Rowman & Littlefield Publishing Group, Inc.
4501 Forbes Boulevard, Suite 200, Lanham, Maryland 20706
www.rowman.com

Unit A, Whitacre Mews, 26-34 Stannary Street, London SE11 4AB

Copyright © 2017 by R. Barker Bausell

All rights reserved. No part of this book may be reproduced in any form or by any electronic or mechanical means, including information storage and retrieval systems, without written permission from the publisher, except by a reviewer who may quote passages in a review.

British Library Cataloguing in Publication Information Available

Library of Congress Control Number: 2017955318

∞™ The paper used in this publication meets the minimum requirements of American National Standard for Information Sciences—Permanence of Paper for Printed Library Materials, ANSI/NISO Z39.48-1992.

Printed in the United States of America

Dedicated to my grandson:
Jacob Jefferson Irwin

Contents

Acknowledgments		ix
Introduction		xi
1	The Importance of Developing Instructional Products, Processes, and Procedures	1
2	Digital and Developmental Instructional Research	15
3	Decision Making in Product Development Research	39
4	Assessment Products that *Might* Contribute to a Useful Science of Education	49
5	Research that *Might* Improve Learning Despite the Traditional Classroom	67
6	The Most Important Instructional Environment (and the Most Difficult to Improve)	85
7	Curriculum Research/Change	93
8	A Big Science Experiment that *Might* Jumpstart the Science's Infrastructure	115
Concluding Thoughts		127
References		131
Index		135
About the Author		137

Acknowledgments

I would like to express my gratitude to Harold Murai, PhD, of the California State University, Sacramento, for his helpful comments on an early draft of the manuscript. Gratitude is also extended to the many, many educational researchers from the past and present whose work influenced this book—scientists too numerous to list and many of whom would probably prefer not to be. However, Edward Thorndike, J. M. Stephens, Doug Ellson, Benjamin Bloom, David Berliner, Betty Hart, Todd Risley, and W. James Popham must be mentioned because of their contributions to the discipline of educational research itself. Finally, I would like to thank Thomas F. Koerner (vice president and publisher) and Carlie Wall (associate editor), and Della Vaché (assistant managing editor) of Rowman & Littlefield for their competent help and support in seeing this project through to completion.

Introduction

This book is the second of two related volumes. The first volume, *The Science of the Obvious*, addressed the following rather impertinent question:

If no educational research had been conducted during this century, would this have deleteriously impacted the American public schools?

To answer this question, twelve genres of educational research were reviewed in order to examine both exemplary and less-than-exemplary studies to provide a reasoned, evidence-based answer. And that answer was, discouragingly:

No.

However, a more important thought question will be proposed for this book, namely:

Is it possible for educational research to develop into a discipline that could constructively impact the education of students?

Assuming a positive answer to this question, an even more important follow-up question would obviously be:

What type of research would be required (and what infrastructural components would be needed) to do so?

Answering this two-pronged question is the basic purpose of *this* book by *embracing* (rather than lamenting) the fact that education truly is a science of the painfully *obvious* and coming terms with the realities that in *this* discipline:

1. Nothing *startling* to rival the theory of general relativity will ever be discovered,
2. Nor will anything be discovered that will substantively increase learning over and above additional relevant instruction.

So what is left? A very great deal if we simply acknowledge these limitations, accept their implications, and adopt a paradigmatic change in the educational research process that migrates away from the creation of isolated, one-and-done research reports toward the creation of *instructional products, processes,* and *procedures* capable of increasing *learning, access to instruction,* and/or *engagement* therewith—and by so doing, develop a discipline more akin to engineering and commercial product development rather than one vainly searching for knowledge for its own sake.

Said another way, this book will propose a radically utilitarian change in the discipline's directional course. And, equally important, the infrastructural components necessary for supporting this shift in priorities will be explored.

This volume will be relatively brief, but it will provide a comprehensive roadmap for creating a science that may be obvious, but that will be *useful* and may even eventually serve to decrease the inequities inherent in our current educational system. For, while the science of education research may be the most obvious of disciplines, its raison d'être involves facilitating what may be society's most important and challenging task—optimizing the education of *all* its young.

After introducing the concept of product development in education accompanied by two seminal examples, one employing a half-century-old effort involving ten sequential experiments and one employing recent state-of-the art digital instruction, a case is made (mirroring society as a whole) that some form of technology-enhanced instruction will constitute the driving force of what is already a movement toward tangible products capable of improving learning, access, or engagement with instruction.

Other suggested avenues of investigation (along with specific study proposals) loosely fit into four categories. The first is infrastructural in nature and involves the assessment products needed to move from a testing system bequeathed to the discipline more than a century ago by the early intelligence test developers. The second proposes instructional products that could improve learning both within (and supplemental to) the traditional classroom. The third and most important of all involves instructional products and processes to facilitate learning within the home environment. And finally, the role of curriculum inquiry, perhaps the most neglected area in educational research, will be considered along with two seminal examples from the discipline's past.

The last chapter presents a "big science" project, the primary purposes of which would be (a) to engage the imagination (and ultimately support) of a public—most of whom aren't even aware that there is such a thing as a science of education—(b) to jumpstart the creation of the infrastructure necessary to create such a science, and (c) to provide a hint regarding the ultimate potential of instruction itself.

A BIT OF HELPFUL BACKGROUND FROM THE PREVIOUS VOLUME

While the contents of this volume are basically independent of the first book, certain assumptions regarding the exclusive subject matter constituting the science of education bear repeating as does a working hypothesis whose etiology and empirical support was presented in that previous work.

First, the totality of the discipline's subject matter is depicted by the following (hopefully self-explanatory) model: Curriculum → Instruction → Learning ≈ Testing, where the equivalence (≈) sign represents the fact that we can only infer that learning has occurred by the testing process.

All of these components are very broadly defined. *Instruction*, besides what goes on in the schools, includes activities such as any form of feedback (such as from testing), listening to and interacting with others (for example, in the crib, at the family dinner table, among peers), self-study, observing and experiencing the environment, reading and being read to, and so on. (Relevance in this context is defined as *instruction that can be understood, is attended to, involves a topic that has not already been learned (or if it has, has not been forgotten), and is assessed by an appropriate test.*) And finally, testing includes all types of assessment methods including observation, oral questioning, and changes in behavior.

The second important holdover from the first volume involves the working hypothesis guiding both it and the present book, which is succinctly stated as:

The only way to increase the amount students learn is to increase the amount of instruction they receive and/or its relevance.

While perhaps not essential background, two informal educational research principles from the distant past (at least in the way this discipline keeps time) that are unfortunately still applied today are:

The Grandmother Principle: One never discovers anything in educational research that their grandmother didn't already know.

The Excrement Principle: Regardless of how promising an intervention's results are, everything turns to excrement once it's introduced into the classroom.

And that's it for background. Let's now address the changes needed to create a useful science of education.

Chapter One

The Importance of Developing Instructional Products, Processes, and Procedures

If the science of education is ever to develop into a meaningful, socially useful endeavor, its researchers must somehow overcome a number of unpleasant realities.

First, we need to recognize the constraints inherent in the traditional classroom model itself, which was dealt with in detail in a book titled *Too Simple to Fail: A Case for Educational Change* (2011) by the present author and will be discussed briefly in chapter 3.

Second, no one needs to be reminded that into today's world *any* proposed change in *any* societal institution will generate a vituperative, social media-driven firestorm of negative reactions and impassioned opinions. And the educational enterprise is certainly no exception, partly because of its importance to such a large proportion of the electorate, partly because public school employees prefer business-as-usual to unproven alternatives, and partly because almost everyone in the public at large has gone to school themselves—thereby engendering a widespread prevalence of perceived (and to a certain extent *actual*) expertise about the schooling process in *everyone* (including parents and politicians).

And finally, as an institution, educational research is as resistive to change as any other. Business-as-usual is less labor intensive, quite lucrative for many, and (partly because the traditional classroom paradigm is so resistant to change) there seems to be nothing educational researchers can do to effect change. (And even if they could do so, there is no guarantee of success because many, many school reforms have come and gone over the past century with little or no impact upon the everyday education of our students.)

So what's to be done? Using the more successful sciences such as physics or biology as models isn't particularly helpful because they have a track record of facilitating the development of useful inventions, therapies, and knowledge for its own sake (all of which have been breathlessly shared by the press and these disciplines' impressive public relations machines, whether accurately or not).

In your author's salad days, for example, the collection and return of moon rocks was ballyhooed as a surefire method of explaining the origin of the universe. Decades later we are assured that multibillion-dollar particle colliders will explain the same thing once we understand just a bit more about God's particle—which may be God himself/herself/itself for all anyone knows.

So with a public relations track record such as this, education can never compete with the natural sciences. Our science also can't discover anything our grandmothers didn't already know. And we certainly can't cure anything—despite occasional bogus neuroscientific claims such as training one's memory via commercially lucrative but ineffective programs relying upon transfer from games designed to provide mental "stimulation" (Melby-Lervåg, Redick, and Hulme, 2016).

At some point educational scientists will need to make a different type of case if they expect to continue garnering their lucrative piece of the public largess. It can't be generating knowledge-for-its-own sake, for what does that even mean with respect to a harried teacher standing in front of a classroom of twenty-five diverse students sitting at their desks? The paying public (at least the ones who know the profession even exists) actually expects the science of education to develop strategies to improve the educational process, not to show that the ceiling tiles in "effective" schools are significantly smaller than those in "less effective" ones (and probably have a lower asbestos content).

This is a goal that the more perceptive members of the discipline understand may be impossible to realize within the current classroom setting, at least based upon past efforts. And even if it were an attainable objective, how could they ever get their discoveries *implemented*? And if they could, well then there's the excrement principle.

But let's set all of that aside, for there's another, even larger impediment to overcome involving a difference in research *orientation*. Investigators in the natural sciences tend to approach their work and conduct their experiments as part of a larger program of research with an eye toward adding to the cumulative knowledge of their particular (often very narrow) subspecialties.

True, they may often (perhaps usually) publish extremely trivial results just as their educational colleagues do, but in most cases their ultimate goal for conducting an experiment isn't to produce stand-alone findings with no planned follow-up regardless of the results. Instead, they have the luxury of believing that, if nothing else, their discoveries will contribute to the cumulative knowledge base of their profession.

Education, on the other hand, is a defiantly *noncumulative* science. Whether planned or not, whether recognized or not, it is composed of a collection of hundreds of thousands of discrete stand-alone studies, published and unpublished. In truth, no one has any idea (or probably cares) how many educational research studies have been published.

What we do know is that the Education Resources Information Center (ERIC), a division of the Institute of Education Sciences, as of early 2017 listed 479,693 research-*related* articles published in the 1,108 journals. The organization also proudly boasts 1.6 million educational articles in its database, which may comprise half of the actual total educational database. And no one anywhere has any idea how many studies have been conducted and placed in the proverbial file drawer *never* to see the light of day.

Surely this is absolute nonsense on a biblical scale. What does it avail anyone to contribute the 1,600,001th article to the ERIC database and have it read perhaps by seven people? Why not instead at least *attempt* to construct a potentially useful educational *product* (which also encompasses processes and strategies) capable of increasing learning, access to learning, or engagement with learning—even if it is used by only seven *students*?

Granted, this will require the adoption of a paradigmatically different mindset, but there is nothing to prohibit those who have created such a product from publishing the fruits of their labors in one of more than a thousand journals to pad their vita, obtain tenure, and thereby ensure biweekly direct deposits throughout their working lives. For in addition to their digitally preserved publications, they will have something *tangible* to mark their research efforts and their professional lives if they are successful in constructing (or inventing) an actual educational *product* someone has (or could have) *used* to learn something.

The remainder of this volume will therefore present two examples of this process. The first is an absolute classic from the discipline's past. And while this cyclical, repetitive discipline seems to possess a great fondness for reinventing the wheel, this particular effort seems to be an exception, perhaps because of the amount of work involved.

So let's journey back into our science's archives to a study conducted more than half a century ago to illustrate what the past has to teach us about the *development* of instructional products via both empirical and nonempirical means. While not realized in their time, the authors' vision (not coincidentally) reflects the spirit of this book's vision of the *future* of the science.

AN EARLY, ARCHETYPICAL EXAMPLE OF THE EMPIRICAL DEVELOPMENT OF AN INSTRUCTIONAL PRODUCT ELLSON, BARBER, ENGLE, AND KAMPWERTH (1965)

This series of experiments was introduced as follows:

> This is a summary report of ten experiments in which the technique of programmed tutoring, applied to the teaching of beginning reading, is developed and given preliminary field tests . . . This paper is properly considered a progress report since the project is not complete; in a sense, it is just beginning. It summarizes the results of ten experiments carried out in a state school for retarded children, in many classrooms of public school systems in Indiana, and in associated laboratory settings . . . These experiments have not been published and it is believed that several of them are not publishable separately. Some are experiments only in the primitive sense of tryouts; in others, a carefully planned design was abandoned in midstream to permit informal investigation of obviously important effects that had not been anticipated in the planning. Such a research strategy, coupled with the relative chaos that characterizes the smoothest-running elementary classrooms [Things haven't changed much in half a century, have they?] in an effective working school, does not always lead to the kind of report that a journal will publish, especially if it is written honestly. But this strategy was appropriate to the aims of the research and to the present state of the art. When ground is first broken in any field of research the effects of some variables are so obvious tests, control groups, or, in some cases, even experiments are not necessary for their detection. (p. 79)

The first study in the series employed a rigidly prescribed paired-associate approach repeatedly coupling words with pictures administered to both children and adults with a mean IQ of 54. The five trials employed took an average of thirty-seven minutes to complete and the average word gain was 11.8 words or 19 words per hour. [Recall that when this study was conducted paired-associate research was still in vogue.]

Presumably encouraged by these results, the investigators next performed an experiment to see if low-IQ students (two adolescents with IQs of 71 and 58, respectively) could successfully serve as tutors—which was reasonable since the paired-associate procedure employed required very little expertise on the part of the tutor. The results were similarly successful but, interestingly, the entire approach was abandoned due to (a) classroom teachers' objections to the use of the mechanistic paired picture-word associations and (b) the investigators' realization that many common words could not be adequately represented by a simple picture. Thus as advertised in their introductory remarks, the investigators weren't hesitant to change directions. [This is not unusual in practice, but to publish one's initial missteps *is* both unusual and potentially helpful to other researchers.]

The new approach, following pilot studies, involved a sight-reading program developed to teach words contained in a sentence. The reading material was printed "on a scroll and presented by a 'teaching machine' [state of the art technology at that time] designed to expose either one sentence alone or one sentence and the words of that sentence in random order." The instructional process involved six presentations, one sentence at a time. The sessions began by presenting an entire sentence and having the subject read it. If read correctly, the tutor reinforced the tutee and proceeded to the next sentence. If an error was made, the sentence was presented again with its constituent words presented below it in random order. The tutor then read the sentence, followed by the tutee reading each word. A specified instructional progression was then followed until both the sentences and the words were read correctly.

The results were positive (in comparison to a non-taught control group), hence the investigators decided to take the next logical step in reading instruction and add comprehension to their repertoire. Two new interventions were added: classroom instruction (in groups of eight students) and alternating instruction (that is, classroom and programmed tutoring). Whether random assignment of tutees was employed is not known but, in any event, the instruction consisted of six half-hour teaching sessions over a one–and-a-half week interval and produced the following results:

As indicated in table 1.1, the authors concluded that alternating tutoring with classroom instruction was significantly more effective than both classroom instruction and control on vocabulary gain while programmed tutoring was significantly superior only to control. No significant differences were observed for reading comprehension.

Table 1.1. Four-Group Programmed Tutoring Study, Experiment IV

Group	Vocabulary Gain	Comprehension Gain	Significant Pairwise Contrasts
Alternating Instruction	37.6	4.1	> Classroom & Control
Programmed Tutoring Alone	32.9	0.9	> Control
Classroom Instruction Alone	18.1	1.5	
Control	6.6	1.3	

Source: Based on table 5 of Ellson, Barber, Engle, and Kampwerth (1965)

The authors concluded that alternating tutoring with classroom instruction was numerically superior to both classroom instruction and programmed tutoring alone although it did not differ significantly from programmed tutoring alone on either indicator. However, this is a hallmark of the type of decisions that must be made in developmental research when a fork in the road is encountered. In this case the investigators probably realized that their product (programmed tutoring) would never replace classroom instruction but instead would be used as a supplement thereto. So they made an executive decision to simply pursue this latter path.

The next experiment consequently contrasted three ways of combining classroom instruction and tutoring versus a no-treatment control while increasing the amount of instruction provided (probably in an attempt to maximize the effect size). The intervention groups were:

1. Tutoring (T) → Classroom (CL) instruction: six T sessions followed by six CL sessions,
2. Six sessions of CL followed by six T sessions (CL → T), and
3. Twelve sessions in which the two modalities were alternated (T & CL).

As indicated in table 1.2, the bulk of the pairwise contrasts involving words learned favored alternating the two modes of instruction (T & CL) although the investigators were less than impressed by their comprehension results. In hindsight they explained these results by suggesting that the poor comprehension results were due to the fact that the students could read less than half of the words in the sentences. (Now as mundane as this conclusion is, many researchers investigating reading comprehension in the past haven't seemed to realize that word recognition is a prerequisite for reading comprehension.)

Table 1.2. Four-Group Study Involving Alternation of Instruction, Experiment V

Group	Vocabulary Gain	Comprehension Gain	Significant Pairwise Contrasts
T & CL (alternating with one another)	57.2	6.6	> Control & CL → T
T → CL (tutoring followed by classroom)	39.0	3.8	> Control
CL → T (classroom followed by tutoring)	37.6	3.7	> Control
Control	12.6	1.4	

Source: Based on table 6 of Ellson, Barber, Engle, and Kampwerth (1965)

The next experiment is quite dated and runs completely counter to our working hypothesis. Here the investigators decided to attempt to find the optimal proportion of reinforcement per unit of material presented for learning based upon B. F. Skinner's edict that reinforcement should be maximized and errors minimized ("by making each successive step as small as possible, the frequency of reinforcement can be raised to a maximum, while the possibly aversive consequences of being wrong are reduced to a minimum"). Recall that the participants were extremely disabled individuals.

Accordingly, forty-one participants were assigned to four levels of targeted proportion of reinforcement (that is, .05, .35, .65, and .95). In other words, for the .35 group, 35 percent of the presented words had previously been answered correctly by the participants on the pretest while group .95 was taught 95 percent of previously learned words. Not surprisingly, the results were relatively linear with the students (Ss) who were taught the fewest words (that is, 5 percent) learning the most, and the Ss who were instructed on 95 percent of the words learning almost no new words.

The investigators were apparently surprised by these findings, since the results didn't reflect Skinner's principle. Why this would be surprising is somewhat unclear since, on average, group 1 Ss were taught more than four times as many words as group 4 Ss. This is hindsight, however, and an example of how scientists can be blinded by the paradigm within which they work.

The next rather complex study was designed to "evaluate a revision of the sight-reading program with particular concern for the feasibility of its continued use over an extended period of time (two 20-minute sessions per week for 12 weeks)" in addition to investigating retention and transfer. (The latter was found to be problematic as it always is.)

However, satisfied with their program for teaching sight-reading/word recognition, the investigators moved on to further investigate the more challenging task of increasing reading comprehension. The purpose of this experiment therefore "was to try out three programs designed to teach comprehension of simple instructions." The "programs" consisted of the following three comprehension components (which were not compared to one another, but together would comprise the authors' total comprehension intervention):

1. The presentation of one-page units involving "a picture with two or more objects, a sentence describing the picture, and a second instruction-sentence or question that could be responded to appropriately by pointing to one of the objects."

2. The same materials were employed with the "instruction-sentence or question" being deleted and replaced by oral questions followed by the Ss pointing to and reading the correct answer via a sort of multiple-choice item.
3. Similar to the second approach "except that correct answers could not be obtained from the accompanying illustration, but only from a statement that preceded the question."

The authors concluded that the comprehension results were promising (they also interviewed students who appeared to enjoy the activities involved), although they apparently did not reach statistical significance as compared to control. However they concluded that the results for the alternation of tutoring and classroom-instruction group supported the findings from previous work, although there was a high attrition rate for this group and of course instructional time was not controlled.

Recognizing the limitations of the sight-reading of whole words for ultimately building a large reading vocabulary, the final developmental experiment was designed to try out a word-analysis/phonics program consisting of (a) eight initial/final consonant sounds and (b) five short vowel sounds in three-letter consonant-vowel-consonant words. The two treatments consisted of two sessions per day for a six-week period. The first intervention was devoted to the sight-reading and comprehension instruction as just described, while the second intervention consisted of both sessions being given over to phonics instruction followed by the completion of a nine- or ten-sentence story taught with the sight-reading and comprehension approaches. The results were somewhat disappointing and the authors concluded that most of the children were not prepared for the word-analysis program and that the experiment was too short to include both preparation and sufficient time on the program to evaluate it.

The final experiment was aptly titled *A Preliminary Field Test of Programed* [sic] *Tutoring as a Supplement to Classroom Teaching*. Toward this end, two groups were contrasted. An experimental group composed of a classroom of thirty-four Ss and a control group containing thirty-four matched Ss (on the Metropolitan Readiness Test) from four other classrooms in the same school. The control group consisted of instruction in the regular curriculum; the experimental group consisted of two fifteen-minute tutoring sessions per day for twelve weeks.

An attempt was made to schedule the tutoring sessions when the affected students would normally be working on individual reading assignments scheduled by the classroom teacher. Tutors were homemakers who received twelve hours of training, but had had no former teaching experience or training. (It is interesting that Popham [1971] later used homemakers [along with some other nonprofessional group] and compared them to trained, experienced teachers, finding no difference with respect to the amount of classroom learning elicited.) The results were quite heartening for the programmed tutoring intervention group significantly outperformed the control group on a standardized test, a word-analysis test, and word recognition.

The authors ended their long article by concluding that their program resulted in learning among students who have the most trouble learning to read and that the strategy worked best as a supplement to classroom teaching. They also encouraged other researchers to engage in more developmental work of this nature.

This conclusion is now incontrovertible with the effects of tutoring having been demonstrated multiple times in subsequent years. The authors' call for more developmental work, while perhaps not falling on completely deaf ears, has gone largely unheeded over the succeeding decades and sadly this seminal study has been all but forgotten with the passage of time.

While this study was undoubtedly described in unpalatable detail for many readers, it constitutes a logical direction that the science of education *might have taken* but, with a few exceptions, did not. It also serves as an unfortunately rare illustration of using a research program to *develop* (as opposed to simply *evaluate*) a product, so let's examine some characteristics of this study (and approach) that distinguish it from a stand-alone, one-and-done educational experiment.

1. As the authors noted, the majority of the ten experiments couldn't have been published separately. This is partly because all of the studies were underpowered (and even worse, many correspondingly failed to reach statistical significance), and partly, quite frankly, because several were poorly designed (for example, random assignment was not quite the mandated gold standard in those days that it is now).
2. However, not having to worry about publishing each study individually gave the investigators the freedom to explore options and make decisions on the fly. This approach was therefore much closer to actual laboratory bench work, where a series of experiments involving "small" procedural questions precedes anything likely to be published.
3. Relatedly, it also gave the investigators the freedom to "fail" in any given experiment. Few stand-alone experiments are conducted to see if something that does "work" can be *improved upon*—partly because of the effort involved, the likelihood of failure, and the self-imposed need to conduct only publishable experiments (that is, experiments accompanied by comforting p-values below 0.05—more on this in chapter 3).

Replication: Fortunately there is a happy ending to this story, for there was a follow-up study conducted a few years later, again under the leadership of Professor Ellson with Phillip Harris as the project director (Ellson, Harris, and Barber, 1968). This experiment was designed as a final, more controlled evaluation of the programmed-tutoring product as compared to the previously abstracted study which employed usual instruction as its control.

In contrast, in the 1968 study the investigators were primarily interested in ascertaining (a) if the amount of tutoring could be reduced and still exert a salutary effect and (b) if it was necessary to structure tutoring to the extent done by the programmed method.

Toward those ends, participants were drawn from the first-grade classrooms of twenty inner-city schools and ten pairs of students from each were matched on certain key variables. Then, within each matched pair, one school was randomly assigned to "expert-designed" (direct) tutoring and the other was to receive programmed tutoring. Students within schools were then assigned to receive one versus two sessions per day, with a control student drawn from the same classroom and matched (on the Metropolitan reading readiness test) with each tutored student.

Without going into excruciating detail, programmed tutoring resulted in significantly more learning in comparison to direct tutoring, and two sessions per day of programmed tutoring produced significantly more learning than one session per day. The investigators appeared to be rather surprised with the failure of direct ("expert-designed") tutoring since, during the course of the study, both tutors and students seemed to be especially enthusiastic about this type of instruction (that is, "a good time was had by all"). Professor Ellson, however, was understandably quite pleased with the results and was confident that he could improve his product through continuation of the same developmental process.

Unfortunately, like just about everything else from educational research's past, Professor Ellson's work was destined to be forgotten. However, the project's director of this final evaluation (Professor Ellson is deceased) gave this appraisal of his mentor's retrospective on the program in response to an email I sent him (which he kindly gave me permission to publish):

> *What a delightful email to read this morning. Dr. Ellson has passed several years ago, but I remained in close contact right to the end of his life. His biggest disappointment was that the only way for Programmed Tutoring to survive was to turn it over to the private sector. This was something that was so offensive to him that he just couldn't sell all his work for others to profit. He felt that the public money made his work possible and the fact that the research data wasn't sufficient to make the change more permanent [was disappointing I think Phillip*

meant]. He had very high standards for research and had difficulty in dealing with leaders who thought expert opinion was sufficient.

That particular article was cited several times as the most outstanding example of quality research being done in the public schools. Unfortunately, the quality of the research and the rigor of the findings and the social implications didn't seem as important in the late '60s.

There is hardly a day that goes by that I don't reflect on what might be if we were to bring this out today, and you are absolutely correct in how humble Dr. Ellson was, but when he came running down the hall of the Psychology Building screaming my name and hollering that the data is in and Programmed Tutoring came out best . . . We had a lot of fun over his reaction but he gave me all the resources I could use to put together a test for his tutoring process; and when he observed the sessions he too had concluded that Directed Tutoring looked like it was doing more for students. However, the data said otherwise. This was a major turning point in my own career and it made it clear to always wait for the data.

Thanks again for the flood of great memories this morning and don't hesitate to contact me if you have further questions about Doug Ellson.
Cordially
Phillip Harris, EdD
Executive Director
AEC

Far be it for the present author to criticize one of his heroes, but in retrospect one wonders if Professor Ellson erred in *not* commercializing his product. Granted those were different times (the heart of the 1960s) with different world views. However, as will be discussed later, from a purely product-development, scientific perspective, sometimes it is incumbent upon scientists to market their product and not to hide their light under a basket. Professor Ellson and his team's work received several well-deserved awards at the time but, in the present author's opinion, the product and the process by which it was developed were worth far more than such fleeting recognition.

A MUCH MORE RECENT EXAMPLE OF AN EXEMPLARY PRODUCT DEVELOPMENT PROJECT

Let's now jump from the twentieth to the twenty-first century and consider a very modern version of the type of educational product and developmental effort that will undoubtedly revolutionize instruction and learning. For, as will be discussed in the next chapter, it is difficult to visualize any meaningful educational product developed during the remainder of this century that does not involve some form of digital or otherwise technologically enhanced instruction.

COMPUTER-GUIDED ORAL READING VERSUS INDEPENDENT PRACTICE

This study (Mostow, Nelson-Taylor, and Beck, 2013) compared an automated "Reading Tutor" to a silent reading control, which, let's face it, is equivalent to instruction versus no instruction, so we know how the results will come out (but that's true of 95 percent of educational research studies). What makes this study both interesting and important is the development and employment of voice recognition software to teach a wide variety of reading skills: word recognition, cursory phonetic word attack skills, the spelling of new words, and reading comprehension.

The mainstay of the program, however, was the ability of a digital product to allow students' oral reading of books, both of their own and the program's choosing (the latter normally selecting texts the students had not read previously and that were slightly above their reading level). The computer was programmed to supply words that the students did not know, which was triggered by their pausing on a word for a given length of time, reading the word incorrectly, or clicking a mouse on a word they didn't know. Frequent review and testing also took place.

In addition to strategies involving students reading text displayed on the computer screen, some of the additional instructional processes included:

1. Prompting students to spell new words that were previewed prior to reading a story,
2. Allowing students to tailor some of their instruction by choosing a wide variety of activities (the choice of the story to read being one as well as allowing younger children "to create new stories by choosing a series of words and phrases that the Reading Tutor then used to fill in blanks in a story template"),
3. Allowing students to write their own stories and read it to the Reading Tutor, and
4. Reinforcing "spelling to sound mapping."

One hundred ninety-three suburban students were randomly assigned to use the Reading Tutor or to read silently for twenty to twenty-five minutes per day for seven months. The students assigned to the Reading Tutor significantly outperformed their silent reading counterparts on word recognition, blending words, and spelling, and manifested a "trend" toward superiority on several more tests.

Previous studies by the investigators had shown superior gains in students' reading comprehension when they were taught by the Reading Tutor as compared to usual classroom instruction (Mostow, Aist, Huang, et al., 2008), although a trial comparing human tutoring to the Reading Tutor (Mostow, Aist, Burkhead, et al., 2003) found the former superior on a "Word Attack" measure but equivalent (and superior to a control group) on other reading measures. (This latter finding suggesting equivalence between digital and human tutoring, incidentally, would be quite impressive if it replicates.)

Besides the more than ten years of developmental work that went into this product, one of the most impressive components of the investigators' work was their quality improvement research (which the authors referred to as data mining) in which automated mini-experiments were conducted during the course of the year employing only the Reading Tutor students. Different methods of introducing new words were contrasted, for example, as were alternative methods of review and numerous other components of the program. Equally important, Reading Tutor students were administered frequent affective measures to ascertain the popularity of different program components since palatability would be expected to translate to engagement (especially in a context in which an unsupervised reader accessed the product). These affective measures incorporated both constructed responses (for example, "It was fun" versus "It was okay" versus "It was boring") as well as open-ended comments such as:

> I like reading with the computer because when you don't know a word, you can click on it.
> You can't click on your teacher. (p. 252)

But a good time was not had by all as witnessed by a first grader's response to the question, "What do you think you've learned from using the Reading Tutor?" (Students gave their answers orally and the program recorded them.)

> That computers are the dumbest thing I've ever known in the whole universe that's what I learned; that the reading tutor I mean that reading on the computer can annoy you because . . . the computer always hates you. (p. 272)

Implications: As will be discussed in the next chapter, this is exactly the type of work the discipline needs more of: the development of digital instructional products that provide alternatives or supplements to a teacher standing in front of a classroom. This study also illustrates the potential for the developmental process itself, not to mention the improvement of the product once implemented since digital instructional materials can always be improved and will periodically need updating due to curricular changes.

This team's use of automated mini-experiments conducted as part of the data collection process also constitutes a remarkable innovation that could eventually revolutionize not only product developmental research but become an exemplary genre of investigation in its own right. Perhaps this genre could eventually even employ classic experimental and quasi-experimental designs such as fractional factorial designs and balanced incomplete-block designs (Bausell, 2015) that have historically been only practical for industrial product development.

Inevitably voice recognition and other digital technologies will continue to improve exponentially due to other marketplace developments, thereby reducing the need (and expense required) for the intensive preliminary work involved in this and other past digital instructional work. And while this work by Mostow and his colleagues is in many ways seminal, there is an increasing amount of work being conducted in other subject matters and with other iterations of digital tutors.

As only one example, Ward, Cole, Bolaños, et al. (2013) describe a product they developed called My Science Tutor (MyST), with a virtual tutor named Marni whose head and face movements were synchronized with a prerecorded human voice. The product was evaluated against both a no-treatment control and small-group instruction. It outperformed the control group and was impressively found to be equivalent to small-group instruction. (Impressive because while human tutoring has been shown to be more effective than small-group instruction involving two to five students, small-group instruction involving both two and five students has been shown to be more effective than classroom instruction [Moody, Bausell, and Jenkins, 1973].)

Both the reading tutor and the science tutors were extremely labor intensive to develop, partly because of the state-of-the art of digital voice recognition software available when their developmental efforts began. However with the advances in digital technology made since the turn of the century, developmental research involving digital instructional products will require the adaptation of existing technology rather than the creation of anything not already in everyday use.

Chapter Two

Digital and Developmental Instructional Research

Surely one of the least controversial predictions possible concerning the future of education is that technology will eventually play a much larger role than it presently does. This will occur *despite* the best efforts of many researchers, teachers, school administrators, and school of education faculty, all of whom will need to engage in some degree of retooling.

This change will occur (and is occurring) due to the truly remarkable degree to which digital innovations have permeated (and will continue to permeate) society itself. From an educational perspective, among other things, it will involve the ever-increased utilization of digital instruction. The ultimate transformation of the schooling process (which among societal institutions is second only to religion in its imperviousness to change) will ultimately be facilitated by the remarkable confluence of two otherwise independent sources:

1. The increased use of digital instruction in the classroom will eventually make the teacher's job more palatable and less labor intensive.
2. The remarkable extent to which digital instruction shares the almost identical mechanisms of action with tutoring, the most effective (but far from the most cost efficient) form of instruction known.

Where all of this will lead, no one knows. However, along with the automated possibility of product improvement experiments, the transcription of the curriculum to a variety of digital formats constitutes the most innovative and promising work in the field of education—both from the perspective of increased learning *and* increased access to instruction. And while this work may appear more akin to the processes engaged in by software and hardware startups than what we have traditionally thought of as educational research, it is exactly the type of work the science of education needs.

Before discussing these issues further, let's consider one possibility of what a more digitally intense instructional paradigm might look like in the near future. This vision involves something a bit more radical than anything actually existing today, but all of its technological requisites have already been developed in other arenas for other applications.

A VISION OF THE CLASSROOM OF THE NEAR FUTURE

Everyone involved with the schooling process is acutely aware of the learning impediments inherent in the traditional classroom model consisting of one teacher standing in front of twenty-five to thirty students with diverse learning needs, heroically attempting to fulfill as many (but never all) of them as possible. And almost everyone involved with the schooling process would agree that far and away the most efficacious alternative to this model would consist of supplying every child with a personal tutor, but this is obviously infeasible.

The next best option would therefore appear to be the construction of an alternative or *intensive supplement* to the traditional classroom capable of at least *simulating* the tutoring paradigm. The rationale for such a system would be the same as the one that generated our present, relatively efficient (but certainly less-than-optimally effective) mode of schooling: providing universal, equitable education to society's youth.

Until very recently the traditional public school classroom instruction remained basically unchallenged because of its primary advantages: economy of scale and manageable manpower requirements. However, that was then and this is *now*. Factories are no longer populated by thousands of workers performing menial and mind-numbing tasks such as welding widgets together. Instead these jobs are increasingly performed by individuals overseeing machines that oversee other machines that perform the actual assembly behaviors. Why then should we employ college-educated teachers to ask students what $4 + 7$ equals or what CO_2 stands for?

Is it really so difficult to reconceptualize our standard image of a single teacher standing in front of twenty-five to thirty students and shift to a new paradigm where a group of students is sitting in front of computer monitors (or tablet-type devices embedded in their desktops) equipped with headsets? Can we envision a setting:

- Where each student is busily working on extremely specific learning objectives whose instruction is delivered via software designed solely to ensure mastery of those objectives?

- Where instruction is tailored to each student's needs, as determined by constant, individualized testing (which is also solely objective-based)?
- Where testing only what is taught is so unobtrusive and of such brief duration that it puts the "Response to Intervention" concept to shame?
- Where testing does not occur only at year's end but goes on constantly throughout the school *day* to determine (a) which instructional objectives from the day's lessons (or each individual student's learning profile) have or have not been mastered and (b) which instructional objectives each student will need to be taught next?
- Where testing results are seamlessly recorded and compiled into a permanent digital record, easily accessed and analyzed?

One such model was previously proposed as a schooling innovation in *Too Simple to Fail* (Bausell, 2010), but its implications are equally revolutionary for the science of education. And as witnessed by the Reading Tutor example presented in the previous chapter, its implementation for both purposes becomes more inevitable each year. So consider the following possibility.

At the rear of the room, perhaps on a raised platform, sits a learning technician (teacher, for those who prefer tradition) thoroughly trained in digital technology (not the irrelevant pap consuming so much of the university-based college of education curriculum or commercial workshops). In front of this learning technician are several monitors on students' desks capable of providing split-screen views of as many individual student screens as necessary at any given point in time.

The technician's raised seat is also positioned to provide visual contact with each student and to bring any misbehaving students back on task (which can be done individually through the headphones without disrupting the entire class). The room is also equipped with cameras, both to facilitate this process and to provide an early-warning system of potentially disruptive behavior (or other forms of noncompliance including any displayed by the learning technician) to a centralized observation deck for the school as a whole. Each student's computer has software that permits constant monitoring by the learning technician and provides automatic notification when responses aren't keyed in (or screens changed) within a given period of time.

Students are encouraged to ask the technician for any pertinent directions or help, either via the microphones in their headsets or by instant messaging, but no communication (oral or digital) is permitted between students unless it constitutes a planned part of the lesson. (The latter restriction is designed to reduce disruptive behavior, which can further be minimized by changing desk configurations or with the judicious placement of visual blocks between desks as needed.) An aide could also be present to facilitate student learning by answering questions or delivering brief in-person tutorials. If this latter resource proves too expensive, a backup online "help desk" would be available to answer student queries and possibly to schedule small-group in-person sessions for students experiencing unusual difficulties with the same objectives. Peer (or upper grade) tutors might also be employed to deliver similar remedial help after school.

Because the entire year's curriculum (indeed, the entire elementary, middle, and possibly high school curricula) is now broken down into discrete instructional objectives, all students' individual progress on these objectives would be saved in a database to which they, their parents, the learning technician, and school administrators have access. All students progress at their own rate, no one is held back due to the progress of the overall class, and remedial face-to-face tutoring or small-group instruction is provided to those individuals who appear to be progressing more slowly than they should or than they or their parents would like. (To stay in business, commercial, extra-school tutoring services would need to employ the same objectives students were having trouble with and would be supplied the necessary information with parental consent.) Also, no one would be forced to move on to subject matter for which the necessary prerequisites had not been mastered.

Of course, some students will always either fail to thrive or learn at slower paces than others, but at least they would no longer be required to wait up to six months to be assigned to special education classes of questionable efficacy (since their lack of progress would be documentable in a very brief time frame). Every aspect of instruction would be transparent and easily accessible.

All objectives, lessons (which might be composed of a single objective or a cluster thereof) and sample tests could also be available on a website to permit parents (or their designees, such as for-profit tutoring services—remote or in person) to provide extra-school opportunities for children to (a) progress faster, (b) receive instruction on enrichment topics, or (c) obtain specifically targeted remedial instruction. The basic mode of instruction in this approach would be test, teach, retest, and repeat the entire process until an objective is mastered or, if this fails, to earmark the objective for future work and go on to another objective for which the problematic objective is not an absolute prerequisite.

Review would also be periodically administered to address forgetting, identified via brief, periodic retesting. Full-scale, comprehensive subject-matter tests would be objective-based and would be administered at the beginning *and* end of the school year (if grade level, age, and the school calendar retain any particular relevance at all). The actual items and the specific instructional objectives used on these summative tests would not be available to anyone (students, parents, or school personnel) prior to their administration.

The sheer number of instructional objectives taught during the course of an entire year would require some sort of sampling approach for the summative test with adaptive measures employed to avoid frustration on the part of students who have not progressed far enough in the curriculum to have been exposed to each and every instructional objective (or to waste the time of those for whom the majority of the "easier" objectives had obviously been mastered). But even the process (for example, randomized or stratified by difficulty or importance) by which objectives are chosen for the comprehensive tests would be totally transparent and the full set of objectives (but not the specific summative-test items) would be available to all interested parties.

Rather than being designed simply to rank-order students, these tests would be engineered to provide estimates of the proportion of instructional objectives (or instructional units) mastered at any given grade level. In addition, the *difference* between the beginning and the end-of-year comprehensive tests could be used to more validly evaluate individual learning laboratories, schools, school districts, and states if desired.

An additional advantage to this process is that everyone everywhere would hopefully eventually employ the same (or compatible) technology, thereby reducing its cost and greatly simplifying troubleshooting. However the most useful aspect of the entire instructional system would be the ease with which it and its instructional modules could be improved, revised, and amplified as compared to traditional paper-based textbooks and manuals.

The proportion of the curriculum that would be computer-based is impossible to predict. Certainly didactic group lessons would still be delivered for certain topics, both to vary day-to-day routines and because they may prove to be more effective or popular for certain topics. The same holds for class discussion and lectures, although some analog to social media might be employed.

DVDs will probably be extinct by then, but YouTube or its equivalent is already being used for educational purposes and a special site could be reserved for approved content. Existing forms of digital communication (blogs, Twitter, Facebook, and modalities that will continuously develop) might also be adapted for purely educational purposes.

Regardless of the specific instructional methods employed, however, the heart and soul of this model would consist of:

1. An explicitly detailed curriculum,
2. The availability of computerized instructional materials to teach every concept covered in the curriculum,

3. Transparent tests designed to assess this curriculum and only this curriculum, and
4. Potentially most importantly of all (especially for reducing learning disparities due to previous instructional time limitations), the online 24/7 availability of all of this material to enable students, parents, or their designees to engage in as much additional self-study (including the availability of enrichment topics) or instructional time as they choose at the time of their choosing.

Completely impractical, demented ravings of a geriatric researcher you ask? Perhaps, and certainly a few years off, but does anyone doubt that some version of this vision will eventually be part of the schools of the future? And if so, shouldn't the development of the necessary infrastructure be a prime objective of the educational research agenda of the *present*?

Isn't it, after all, "nothing" more than an extension of the tutoring paradigm—the first instructional method ever employed and the most effective yet invented? Let's count the ways that the two modalities share the same mechanisms of action.

SIMILARITIES OF THE LEARNING MECHANISMS BETWEEN DIGITAL AND HUMAN TUTORING

Mechanism #1: *A human tutor can efficiently ascertain exactly what the tutee has and has not learned by simple questioning.* Couldn't a computer accomplish the same thing via constant, single-item testing of key objectives? In fact, this is one of the few aspects of digital tutoring that is potentially superior to its human parent version because of both the speed with which testing can be conducted and the ease with which the results can be stored for future reference.

Certainly a classroom teacher *could* also assess what his or her students know prior to beginning an instructional episode and after its completion, but this is seldom practical. It is disruptive and time-consuming and even if teachers had access to current technology (for example, a classroom response system) to immediately score their classes' responses to questions and provide feedback regarding correct or incorrect answers, this would waste the time of those students who already knew the content being taught.

Computerized instruction, on the other hand, can quickly administer brief quizzes anytime (at the beginning, middle, and/or end of a tutoring session) and tailor instruction specifically to what individual students haven't yet learned. It is criminal that teaching students only what is *relevant* and providing students with as much instructional time as they personally need to learn constitutes a radical concept in education—especially since we currently have the capability of programming a computer to use adaptive testing and to tailor instructional content to individual students' needs.

Mechanism #2: *A tutor spends less time in maintaining discipline and hence is able to deliver more instruction.* Surely the carefully monitored digital classroom described above possesses the same advantage with each student having a monitor staring at him/her upon which a task is displayed specifically tailored for his/her learning needs. Wouldn't this make it more difficult to talk to one's neighbors or display attention-getting behaviors in the presence of earphones designed to block out extraneous noise?

Of equal importance, time-wasting, time-honored (and often irritating) traditional classroom practices such as listening to other classmates asking irrelevant questions about the lesson (at least irrelevant to that portion of the class that already knows the answer) would be eliminated. Also eliminated would be the practice of teacher queries delivered to random students (or downtime while the teacher chooses among a sea of upraised arms).

True, some adherents to Lev Vygotsky's theories espoused more than a half-century ago might object that the social aspects of learning would be minimized in such a setting. It could be argued, on the other hand, that most of the social interactions that go on in the current classroom setting are detrimental (or at least not conducive) to *learning*. Also, whenever human beings are involved in a common activity in close proximity to one another, social interactions will inevitably arise. And if they don't, such interactions can be purposefully organized.

Mechanism #3: *Wouldn't a learning laboratory simulate a tutor's ability to focus students' attention exclusively upon instruction?* True, there is no tutor sitting directly across from the student, but there is a computer screen situated on the learning technologist's desk upon which each student's tasks are displayed and which requires direct responses from the student and returns immediate feedback thereupon.

It is also worth repeating that each student's screen would be directly observable (in the learning technician's line of sight or electronically via the click of a mouse). The learning technician could also ascertain when anyone's attention begins to waver or daydreaming commences by the lack of electronic responses to the interactive instructional software. The technician could then ascertain if the student didn't understand something, simply needed to have his/her attention refocused, or required rest or an alternative task (all of which could be addressed via personal oral communication using the earphones or by simply going over to the student's desk).

Most importantly, all of this could be done without disrupting anyone else in the classroom and would certainly be less disruptive than classroom teachers' periodic admonitions to students to be quiet. Of course it could be argued that the learning technician, by the nature of the role, would have less of a formative impact upon children than do current tutors or teachers.

Whether or not this is true is not known, but if it is, it might not be such a bad thing. Haven't we all had about as many teachers who had negative as positive affective impacts upon us?

Mechanism #4: *Wouldn't this genre of instruction, tailored as it is to students' needs, be almost as personalized as occurs in the tutoring model?* This is not meant to suggest that the digitally driven instructional laboratory envisioned here would be as effective as instruction administered one-on-one by a competent adult tutor. Human tutoring of this sort is a benchmark that is unlikely to ever be surpassed.

What is being suggested, however, is that with considerable developmental work and creative thinking, digital instruction might come in as a close second. It may even prove to have a few advantages of its own, such as the speed with which it can test students and the capability it provides to automatically track and record their personal progress. Decisions can also be made automatically and nonarbitrarily regarding which objectives need to be taught next, somewhat like the different levels of a video game where the successful completion of each stage is not only rewarding in and of itself, but also brings with it the built-in challenges and satisfaction of having gained access to the next level.

Also like a video game, students will become *very* adept at negotiating this type of instruction through extensive practice using the same icons and standardized procedures. (And don't forget that testing—especially with immediate feedback—*is* instruction.)

Mechanism #5: *Wouldn't digital students feel free to ask more questions directly related to their learning than students in a traditional classroom setting, thereby simulating another advantage of human tutoring?* Anyone who has taught in the classroom model knows that some students ask far more questions than others, and some never ask any instruction-related questions. Overall, the frequency of student-generated classroom questions appears to be quite low (Good, Slavings, Harel, and Emerson, 1987), while the opposite has been found to be true for human tutoring as illustrated by the following study:

DEMONSTRATION OF ONE OF THE ETIOLOGICAL ASPECTS OF THE SUPERIORITY OF THE TUTORING PARADIGM

This descriptive study (Graesser and Person, 1994), whose first author is one of the giants of educational research employing technology and multimedia learning, provides a relatively rare empirical assessment of yet another potential mechanism underlying tutoring's superiority compared to classroom instruction. The study investigated the frequency and types of student questions asked in tutoring sessions based upon the belief that student questioning during instruction plays an important role in learning. (The authors also cite studies that have shown that "improvements in the comprehension, learning, and memory of technical material can be achieved by training students to ask good questions.")

Three barriers to student questioning are hypothesized: (a) identifying what students do not know; (b) the potential loss of social status by admitting ignorance or asking a bad question; and (c) not possessing good question-asking skills. The tutoring paradigm was hypothesized to reduce all three barriers. [All of which, incidentally, should also be minimized in a digitally enhanced classroom.]

Two groups of participants were used: twenty-seven undergraduate students enrolled in a research methods course and thirteen seventh-grade students identified by their teachers as needing help in their algebra class. Three graduate students tutored the former sample and ten high school students the latter.

Tutoring sessions were transcribed and exhaustively categorized (for example, with respect to degree of specification, content, quality) for both tutees and tutors with reasonable degrees of interrater reliability. The average rate of students' questions for the two samples was 26.5 per hour and according to the investigators:

> given that the classroom-questioning literature estimates that a particular student asks .11 question per hour in a classroom setting, the incidence of student questions during tutoring is approximately 241 times the incidence of student questions in classroom settings (from the perspective of a single student). Based upon course exams, the authors concluded that "student achievement was positively correlated with the quality of student questions after students had some experience with tutoring, but the frequency of questions was not correlated with achievement." (p. 104)

The true contribution of this study, however, involves its demonstration of another important etiological reason for tutoring's impressive effectiveness. And while the availability of a learning technologist in the digitally enhanced classroom will undoubtedly not be able to match the degree of questioning found for human tutoring in this study, the ability of students to ask questions anonymously should reduce one of the three barriers discussed above. If needed, a built in remote "instructional help desk" option should also help.

WHY DIGITAL RATHER THAN FACE-TO-FACE TUTORING THEN?

First and most obviously, while human tutoring may be indicated for certain types of students with severe past instructional deficits or organic problems, it obviously isn't practical as a mainstream instructional medium for everyone. Second and perhaps not quite as obvious, since tutors are normally unsupervised and can do whatever comes easiest to them, they are free to do whatever they please. Digital tutoring, on the other hand, responds to variations in performance due to tutor fatigue or noncompliance (hence quality control is assured, at least for the instructional content).

BUT WHAT ABOUT THE HUGE DEVELOPMENT INFRASTRUCTURE REQUIRED FOR DIGITAL TUTORING?

The process of developing such an infrastructure is not as daunting as it may appear. First, its total replacement of traditional classroom instruction is neither necessary nor wise, thus it doesn't need to occur full blown like Athena leaping from her father's head. And since digital tutoring already exists as a supplemental adjunct to classroom instruction in many sites, different components of the above vision can be introduced piecemeal.

HARDWARE

Ultimately the student computers could be extremely cheap, limited machines that did little more than access the servers (or that portion of the Internet) set aside for its instructional purposes. Spare computers should be available within the classroom and a malfunctioning machine should be capable of being reconnected by the learning technician in a matter of minutes. And of course everything in the system would need to be backed up and there should be backups for the backups.

SOFTWARE

This would be the most difficult component of the entire system because the *same*, agreed-upon software would need to be employed that was completely compatible with Word and Excel and a similarly agreed-upon programming language, otherwise a Tower of Babel would result as historically occurred when schools and hospitals first began to respectively use computers (a) for primitive digital products and (b) medical records.

For digital learning products, the software should have the capacity of allowing instructional and testing content written in Word or Excel to be simply "dropped" into the program. Obviously too it would need to have quick-testing components capable of branching back to the relevant instructional passages not yet learned or extending to supplemental content.

All of this technology already exists. It is "simply" a matter of putting it all together.

DIGITAL INSTRUCTIONAL MODULES OR UNITS OR CURRICULA

Nowhere is the inseparability of our four-component model of education (Curriculum → Instruction → Learning ≈ Testing) more apparent than for digital instruction. Optimally, instructional objectives would be written for the entire public school curriculum with all digital instructional modules constructed around this convention since it can explicitly define exactly what will be taught and what will be tested.

Once a critical mass of modules has been developed or adapted and the software is sufficiently user friendly, the process could be opened up to the professional community as a whole. In addition to converting the entire public school curriculum into a supplementary or alternative digital repository, members of different professions could be persuaded to contribute content that they feel might be helpful for students aspiring to join said professions, or to learn what typical members of a profession do on a day-to-day basis.

Perhaps programmers could provide small units on using Python (or whatever the current, most-appropriate programming language at that juncture happens to be) to show students how to instruct the computer to do something that it otherwise wouldn't—or even to create simple games or computational programs for simple algebra.

Or, taking mathematics as only one example, interested professionals could prepare modules for topics not typically taught in the public schools such as counterintuitive probability situations (for example, the likelihood of two students in the same classroom having the same birthday) or "interesting" number theory tricks which might engender a deeper understanding and appreciation for mathematics in general. And if the instructional creation software was sufficiently user friendly (and it would have to be), even someone like your author might create a module or two on experimental design or take a student through the process of conducting a learning experiment with classmates.

It is not difficult to envision the eventual creation of a massive library of digital modules (or even simple YouTube video lessons) that could encompass, supplement, and surpass the official school curriculum. Naturally some mechanism for evaluating the accuracy and appropriateness of the modules would need to be built in via review by content experts.

Once accepted, stored, and made available on a website somewhere, this *instructional* resource might serve as analog to Wikipedia's astounding usefulness for supplying written information. Or better yet, perhaps it could become an adjunct thereof. And from a crucial access perspective (and therefore most importantly of all), these modules would be available free of charge, 24/7.

Obviously this isn't all going to be created overnight and eventually the entire developmental process would need to be coordinated somehow, but not initially and certainly not by some governmental (for example, IES) type contractor. Obviously too, such a resource would constitute an unprecedented increase in international *access* to instruction (which translates to learning) throughout the planet similar to what is presently occurring for online learning.

Who knows what effect this might have upon children? It might well be that the availability of such modules could influence some children's ultimate choice of careers by grabbing their interest and showing them that they can indeed excel in a particular area. Perhaps even children for whom the current educational process holds no interest (and therefore within which they have no future) might find this sort of instruction palatable.

Projects such as these are education's version of respected disciplines such as physics and astronomy whose public relations machines capture the public mind via such respective quixotic quests as finding the smallest possible particle or the origins of the universe—however, the totality of the entire initiative's costs (and everything suggested in this book) would consume no more than a fraction of the cost of a modestly expensive particle accelerator or the existing networks of digitally connected telescopes. In addition:

1. They wouldn't depend upon such disingenuous and extravagant claims as promising as finding a particle capable of creating matter that would then lead to another public relations campaign to find whatever created that particle, and
2. They would create actual *products* capable of positively impacting children's education, which should interest a lot more people than underground tunnels through which invisible subatomic particles race.

This proposed digital educational quest, besides being feasible and in line with existing technological developments, could inform the educational research agenda for generations. Perhaps it could also even supply a direction for school of education faculty with no skills or interest in conducting research.

Many of individuals, for example, have very real skills and interest in curriculum development but there are only so many opportunities available for writing textbooks or similar activities. The same is true for item construction, engaging children's interests, and just plain teaching. And it will be true for inveterate experimenters, once they realize they have nothing to research other than repetitions of past experiments or demonstrations of the obvious. In fact, taking a cue from the Mostow team's Reading Tutor example, quality improvement experiments (automated or individually conducted, learning-based or affective) could constitute a brave new world for researchers given the possibility that they could be built into other teams' product development efforts on a collaborative basis.

DIGITAL TEST DEVELOPMENT

Testing in a digital instructional environment would be a far different process than now routinely occurs in the traditional schooling process. Since testing accompanied by *specific* feedback is a powerful form of instruction, it would go on constantly. Not once at the end of the school year but constantly throughout the school *day*.

Ultimately the purpose of all testing in this or any context is to inform instruction and the basic units of testing in this context are individual instructional objectives. Thus only those objectives, which are not learned, need to be retaught. Naturally this process cannot go on indefinitely for students who chronically fail to master an objective, thus some sort of alternative remediation will need to be worked out. This could be in the form of a digital "cheat sheet" of some sort, since these students will never wander far from their phones or computers.

In addition, twice yearly objective-based summative tests would be administered: once at the beginning of the year, encompassing previously mastered objectives and the objectives projected to be taught during the upcoming school year; once at the end of the school year to assess the amount of learning occurring therein. Obviously some sort of systematic and transparent sampling procedure coupled with adaptive testing would need to be employed.

STUDENT RECORDS

Since the testing unit would be mastery of individual objectives, student records would consequently be far more voluminous than they are presently. However this wouldn't be problematic from a storage perspective given current technology, although perhaps a failsafe (preferably cloud based) backup system should also be employed.

These records would be composed not only of the results of the twice yearly objective-based curriculum tests but of objective-by-objective (and module-by-module) mastery, and perhaps even a record of difficulties and progress toward said mastery could be kept to guide future individualized instructional strategies.

All of this could be recorded for both the official curriculum and *supplementary* curricula since a record of the mastery of both curricula might ultimately become a selection criterion for college entry (certainly an excellent replacement for the SAT) or employment purposes since both would constitute an estimate of student knowledge, industriousness, and engagement. Or alternately, such records might simply constitute a personal indicator of an individual's achievement and self-actualization— a trophy, if you will, of his or her personal efforts during the schooling process and possibly beyond.

RESEARCH POSSIBILITIES

Once student records had been completely denuded of all personal identification information, there is no reason why they could not be stored at a central location for the nation as a whole, thereby permitting careers' worth of data mining for inveterate database aficionados. Such work might even provide information on potential objective-by-objective prerequisites and transfer. Who knows?

FEASIBILITY OF ALL OF THIS

Obviously the hypothetical digital classroom model suggested here is just that, a hypothetical scenario advanced by a single individual. It is quite possible that digital tutoring will never replace classroom instruction or even be a mainstay thereof. Perhaps it will become:

1. An adjunct to classroom instruction like human tutoring,
2. A much-expanded addition to textbook publishers' current digital supplements,

3. A multibillion-dollar for-profit industry in which parents can test their children at home and choose from a menu of instructional objectives upon which their children can receive supplementary digital instruction, and/or
4. A nonprofit service with limited instructional options housed in public libraries or community centers.

Or perhaps it will become another cash cow for school of education researchers to ramp up their salaries by "competing" for funds to conduct the same research studies as their predecessors did within the traditional classroom model.

In any event, the best hope for the development of at least some version of a digital classroom becoming a reality resides in someone like Jeff Bezos, Bill Gates, Mark Zuckerberg, or Larry Page recognizing the modality's full promise (entrepreneurial or philanthropic) and creating a division in their organization dedicated to its fulfillment. But hopefully not to fund:

1. One-and-done studies,
2. An infrastructure that will inevitably disappear as soon as the well dries up, and most certainly,
3. Beltway and university bandits who will spend most of their time and effort applying for the next funding opportunity.

Undoubtedly the biggest impediment to any sensible iteration of a digital instructional future lies in schooling's intractability (aided and abetted by parental conservatism) to all types of change. A close second involves the difficulties inherent in constructing even a working model of some version of the vision just described, for while most of the technological components for a digital classroom have already been developed, no one has come close to putting them together or to developing the necessary infrastructure for a full-scale implementation.

There is therefore no guarantee that the traditional classroom won't be around for a very long time. However a good deal of developmental activity, including digital transcription of a variety of curricula, is presently taking place so something radical this way comes. What it will look like, no one knows.

Whatever that happens to be, even a partial migration to a digital instructional environment will have a major advantage over school reform attempts that have come and gone in the past. In fact, technology may be the *only* siren song strong enough to overwhelm the excrement principle due to its capacity to make it easier for teachers to get through the day and spend less time planning future lessons, and to provide parents with a mechanism by which they can *relatively* painlessly improve their children's school and test performance.

Unanswered questions (which are legion) about the future of digital instruction: One of the most important questions is: how much intensive digital instruction can students tolerate? Human tutoring is a relatively intense experience and, for young students, most studies have employed instructional durations of thirty to forty minutes per session. Of course traditional classroom instruction is also administered in blocks of time (aptly named class periods) that, while a few minutes longer, are probably given over to less than thirty to forty minutes of actual instruction.

Minute-for-minute and hour-for-hour digital instruction has been shown to produce more learning than classroom instruction. Like all types of instruction, however, the more time it can be profitably engaged in, the more learning will occur.

The instructional environment itself may have a major role in increasing engagement. Surely something more ergonomically superior to the average classroom desk can be devised for students engaged in digital learning. So too might changes in:

1. The types and frequencies of breaks (some perhaps employing physical activity),
2. Instructional routines such as the alternation of instructional topics, and/or
3. Modalities of instruction (for example, the use of virtual reality goggles or videos targeting appropriate aspects of the curriculum).

But whatever the instructional specifics turn out to be, a general rule for all instruction (not just digital) is that it should be made as pleasant (or at least as nonaversive) as possible, in order to squeeze as much instruction into the school day as possible, and it should always be accompanied by testing with individualized feedback. So given these parameters and keeping our working hypothesis in mind, let's consider some additional digital instruction questions that need to be answered at some point.

A DIGITAL RESEARCH AGENDA

From a purely research perspective, digital instruction possesses an important advantage over human tutoring in the sense that multiple Ss can be run simultaneously (for example, in a computer lab or remotely) rather than one-at-a-time while maintaining *almost* as much experimental control. Also, using digital instruction as one's research laboratory obviously doesn't require anything nearly as elaborate as the digital classroom described above.

The problem with the truly massive amount of research already conducted on computerized instruction, however, is the same problem bedeviling the rest of the science. It doesn't lead anywhere and it certainly isn't cumulative.

We already know that students will learn regardless of the method by which they are taught so we certainly don't need more demonstrations of that via "no-instruction" controls. Nor do we need more comparisons between classroom and computerized instruction, the most popular digital genre of research undertaken to this point, because such comparisons have no practical or theoretical implications unless (a) the curriculum, (b) the match between the curriculum and the learning outcome, and (c) instructional time (unless time required for mastery or engagement are the dependent variables) are rigorously controlled. This latter point (engagement) requires a quick methodological interlude before it will become an important component of any digital research agenda.

A NOTE ON CONTROLLING INSTRUCTIONAL TIME VERSUS ITS USE AS AN OUTCOME VARIABLE

From a traditional methodological and scientific perspective, the control of instructional time is normally an absolute necessity, especially given the emphasis placed upon it by our working hypothesis. Its control often makes perfect sense when conducting research within the traditional classroom paradigm, since the length of class periods, the school day, and the school year are typically set in stone. And obviously in educational efficacy research contrasting two instructional approaches, if one condition is accompanied by more instructional time than another, it will also be accompanied by a bevy of cherished (but meaningless) p-values below 0.05.

However, at some point in the process of developing an alternative learning environment such as the one being discussed here, it will be necessary to employ time as an auxiliary (to learning) *outcome* variable when (a) it is under the control of the learners or their parents (such as self-study or the completion of homework) or (b) when the goal is to determine which of two strategies is more *efficient* in eliciting mastery of the instructional content. Since digital instruction can theoretically be accessed anywhere students have access to a portal, some research objectives will involve either increasing (a) engagement or (b) the efficiency with which instructional objectives are mastered.

Learning (along with its handmaidens, retention and transfer) will always maintain its preeminent importance and be measured, but some predetermined level of mastery will increasingly serve as the learning criterion and time required thereof as the experimental outcome. There will also be occasions when time itself is purposefully manipulated and thus becomes the intervention of interest (for example, comparing thirty-minute versus sixty-minute instructional intervals to ascertain tolerance or engagement).

Also, with the introduction of more subtle developmental interventions (for example, the introduction of animation within a digital instructional unit versus none), the relative intractability of learning within a fixed interval makes it an even more difficult outcome to differentially influence, both because (a) the auxiliary component may result in a trivial increase in the time needed to navigate through a lesson or (b) the component's primary purpose is to increase the appeal of the learning experience rather than learning itself. (Adolescent boys in particular, for example, are willing to spend untold hours engaged in playing video games, and both genders fill significant portions of their day in digital social media activities.) Or perhaps some research objective might involve clandestinely reappropriating a small proportion of this time to instruction or attempt to make instruction more palatable by involving components of social media.

The specific conceptualization of time's role in these contexts is therefore situationally specific to the investigators' experimental/developmental purposes and ultimate vision of how (and in what environment) their product will be used. What every investigative team must do, therefore, is to carefully weigh the pluses and minuses of either controlling instructional time (broadly defined) or allowing the student to do so.

And when this latter decision is especially difficult, perhaps both options could be compared via a 2 (digital product versus its comparison group) × 2 [(time controlled versus time at the discretion of the student) or (time controlled versus time required to reach a pre-specified level of mastery)] analysis.

POSSIBLE FUTURE STUDIES

So now, with that digression out of the way, let's consider a sampling (and only a sampling) of some of the studies that will result from the development of practically any version of digital instruction designed to be implemented in the public schools. It should be noted that many of these studies are probably product-specific hence their answers must be ascertained for individual digital products.

If the latter is true, no research team will have a life expectancy (or the necessary resources) sufficient to conduct full-blown, fully powered experiments to address those questions relevant to them. Instead, pilot studies or simple observations specific to the product will have to be employed. Hopefully, at some point, pilot studies could be archived somewhere, perhaps in an online, open-access journal dedicated to publishing *all* submissions relevant to the facilitation of future digital work by other teams.

Here then is the promised sample of questions and proposed studies that will undoubtedly arise in the development of digital-learning products (and many other types of instructional product development efforts as well):

1. Are control/comparison groups necessary in the development of an instructional module? It could be argued that in most cases they won't be because we know that relevant instruction begets learning, hence once the instructional software has been developed the real question becomes: *Are the learning objectives adequately achieved by said instruction?* The simplest and quickest way to answer this question is to perform a small-group pretest-module-posttest study and *see*. Again, 100 percent correct performance is usually an unrealistic goal, but an objective-by-objective comparison will ascertain if more emphasis needs to be placed on certain objectives.

   So if an objective is too difficult for the targeted students, options include dropping it or replacing it with another objective. If prerequisite objectives are required (or if the objective simply requires more instructional time), options include increasing the module length or developing a prerequisite module. This process can and should be continued until the investigative team is satisfied with the final results.

2. When control/comparison groups are necessary, what form should they take (for example, usual classroom instruction, small-group instruction, tutoring, remote tutoring, a rival digital-instructional module designed to teach the same content, or even watching a video of a teacher delivering scripted instruction)? Regardless of the choice, the content of the experimental conditions must be standardized to ensure that the assessment instrument is not more closely aligned with one group than the other. Otherwise the experiment is meaningless.

3. What lesson length should be employed? Briefer (for example, a self-contained thirty- to forty-minute session) may be better at the beginning of the developmental process, but this depends upon the curriculum of interest.

4. For lessons that take more than one session, how much intervening time between lessons should be allowed to occur? Should each succeeding

lesson be preceded by a quick review? Or should review be conducted only when intermediary questions cannot be answered?
5. What subject matter should be employed? For elementary school students, math, reading, writing, and science would probably be preferable because of (a) their perceived importance, (b) their topics' affinity to being translated into discrete objectives, (c) the relative ease with which learning measures can be generated based upon these objectives, and (d) their seeming natural amenity to digital instruction. (Writing would appear to be especially amenable to computerized instruction since its feedback—both computer- and human-generated—can be quite detailed and accompanied by track-change notes.)
6. What should be done about objectives that appear to be especially difficult for some individuals? Review, certainly, but at what point should instruction move on to other objectives or topic areas? And if so, what factors should inform such decision?
7. What types of students should be targeted? This decision deserves some thought, since it could be made on investigator preference, characteristics of the particular curriculum employed, availability of participants, or marketing considerations. Instructional experimentation appears to be heavily weighted toward students experiencing learning problems (including those raised in poverty or those with diagnosable learning disabilities). In many ways, this makes sense both from an equity and research perspective. However, unless accompanied by *huge* increases in instructional time, special-education and learning-disabled students will continue to exhibit depressed performance on commercial tests throughout their schooling experience, as witnessed by Jenkins, Dale, Mills, et al., 2006. Of course, one would hope that this could be somewhat ameliorated by digital instruction—although there is no guarantee of this. Thus, the societal impact of better educating our "gifted" students (that is, those who enter school far ahead of their peers because of increased parental instructional time) or our "average" students (that is, those who enter school ahead of their impoverished peers) may be just as great, and hence are viable choices as well.
8. What is the role of homework in such a model? Since many students spend a major portion of their outside-of-classroom lives glued to their smartphones, perhaps completing digital homework assignments thereon could allow the more conscientious of them to look cool while completing their assignments. However it is completed, from a developmental perspective, the role of out-of-class digital assignments should probably be an early investigative target.

9. If time to mastery is chosen as the outcome variable, how should it be defined? The two best-known proponents of mastery learning (John Carroll and Benjamin Bloom) recognized early on that bringing students to a 100 percent mastery level was impractical. One of Bloom's former doctoral students provided evidence that, under certain circumstances, 75 percent was a reasonable criterion (Block, 1972), although this issue needs careful consideration and may be completely situationally specific.
10. Since students will always forget some of what has previously been taught and veridical instruction involves multiple lessons, what should be done about retention from lesson to lesson? How much time and effort should be expended in review? Also, what is the average time differential between original learning and the learning of previously mastered content?
11. *How can engagement be increased and/or extended?* Given our working hypothesis, engagement is basically indistinguishable from relevant time on task when relevance is defined as actually attending to the digital instruction proffered. (In other words, staring at the screen or mindlessly reading the words thereupon does not qualify as engagement.) So can engagement be increased by frequent testing that requires a response on the part of the student, or as previously suggested, by interspersing instruction in another subject-matter area? Is engagement increased by allowing breaks, and if so, what types of activities would be done on the breaks? Exercise? Internet use? Some sort of reinforcement or incentivizing strategy (for example, a brief session in which digital communication with other students is permitted)? Videos (even cartoons) that require no responses to queries? Educational videos of the individual student's choice? Time-limited access to the Internet (with appropriate blocking in place)? Also, do the answers to these questions vary with the subject matter? Do they vary with types of students (for example, while doubtful, perhaps this is an area in which aptitude-by-treatment interactions and/or learning styles might prove to actually *exist*)? Doubtful but possible.
12. The issue of engagement is so crucial in digital learning, in fact, that it may dictate the form and content of almost all digital instructional materials, leading module developers to address the question of how they can persuade students to spend more time therewith. Perhaps very brief (even single item) affective measures can be developed to predict engagement, as well as simply asking students if they would like to access the module in question a second time or observing whether they do or not.
13. What strategies are more effective when an objective is not learned during its initial presentation? Should the same instruction be repeatedly employed or should the objective be taught in a different manner or via a

different modality, such as an instructional hotline? Does it matter *when* it is retaught (immediately versus at some interval later)?
14. What sort of context should be used when a set of objectives is introduced? Should students be provided with age-appropriate information regarding why the objectives are important to learn, where they fit into previous objectives learned, what other topics they are prerequisite for, how this knowledge is applied in various professions, and so forth? Should this context be considered part of the curriculum and tested? (If so, it will need its own associated instructional objectives.)
15. When, and under what circumstances, should content questions be introduced—at the beginning, end, and/or during a session? Should responses be required? What types of questions should be asked? The proposed digital model itself would involve pretesting students to ascertain which objectives are already known but, for research purposes, these items might be administered at other times as well. (Testing, after all, not only informs instruction but is an important modality thereof.) Furthermore, some topics, such as reading comprehension, social studies, or mathematical problem solving, might require completely different types of thought questions than more fact-related content.
16. How might an instructional-digitalization system best facilitate the accessibility of record keeping regarding past and ongoing achievement? What effect might a digitally and automatically updated running score of past objectives mastered have? Could such a score itself help to reinforce engagement or facilitate review if students or their parents were informed when retention assessments would occur?
17. What types of reinforcement (if any) should accompany both original instruction and review in a digital environment, or in other instructional environments, such as homework completion? Are there predictable individual differences in preferences for reinforcement types? If so, are these pervasive (trait) or temporary (state) attributes?
18. How can supplemental digital instruction be effectively integrated with classroom instruction? (We know what will happen to it if its use is left to the "professional judgment" of teachers.) Perhaps a research team could explore the feasibility of how a school-wide, purely supplementary, digitized-instructional laboratory might be constructed and implemented with sufficient fidelity to ensure its use—perhaps beginning with a single set of instructional objectives, or perhaps exclusively for review purposes.

Or as an initial step, perhaps a single school's administration could be cajoled into setting aside a room for translating previous developmental work into a school-based system. (This shouldn't even be attempted until a working model, equipped with a sufficient number of bells and whistles, has been developed for demonstrational purposes.) Or more ambitiously, perhaps a school of education laboratory could be converted or set up for this purpose. (In the case of the latter, a detailed research agenda should be delineated a priori, otherwise long periods of downtime will inevitably occur between projects.)

The potential digital studies just proposed are only a sample of those that could be helpful in the development of digital instructional products. Undoubtedly every research team currently working on such products will encounter unique problems in need of solving. Hopefully in the near future there will be a website or two in which the resulting studies and study ideas can be shared.

In the meantime, however, developmental research of the products themselves typically requires multiple, sequential mini-experiments such as those just tendered. In turn, this procedure requires a different decision making process than those we've come to know and love for stand-alone efficacy studies. So let's consider some of these in the next chapter.

Chapter Three

Decision Making in Product Development Research

The necessity of making directional changes in product development work is a largely underexplored issue in educational research, yet it is an arena within which its practitioners must operate. As the development of the programmed tutoring and reading tutor examples just discussed clearly indicate, developmental products require a journey down a road replete with forks and crossroads in which binary "yes/no," "right/left," or even "revisit" of decisions may be required.

Statisticians past (most notably Sir Ronald Fisher) have bequeathed scientists with a tool of great beauty and utility for making decisions regarding whether a difference, relationship, or hypothesis test is "true" or "false," statistically significant or not, confirmed or not, supported or not, real or not, occurred by chance or not, or however its users choose to portray it. Now set in stone in many disciplines, this decision making convention is of great comfort to researchers and consumers alike.

And it is a useful convention in many ways. True, academicians have been arguing for years about its propriety suggesting various other options or supplements, but the convention has prevailed and will prevail for a long time to come.

Academic researchers have also learned to game the system, which is what *they* do, and understandably so because they must "publish or perish" and $p < 0.05$ has become so entrenched that it is difficult to publish without sprinkling a few into every research report. And this is one reason why so many psychological findings do not replicate (Open Science Collaboration, 2015).

The ultimate purpose of educational product development research, however, is not to secure one's seventy-third publication and then move on to the seventy-fourth. Gaming the system (for example, by employing obviously inappropriate control groups such as "no instruction" or "business as usual") is also counterproductive to this genre of research because the ultimate goal is to create a viable product—not to publish one's *pilot* studies.

So how does one make directional decisions as opposed to terminal ones? The answer isn't completely obvious in this relatively unexplored arena so, in the spirit of transparency, the following options are proposed somewhat tentatively.

The present author is a longtime member of the Church of the $p < .05$ so he cannot bring himself to completely eschew that convention when it is feasible. However, successful inventors in other fields (from software writers to mousetrap developers) have the luxury of trying something out and seeing if it *works*. If it doesn't, then they go back to the drawing board. Certainly they may replicate a strategy, but this involves time, materials, or rodents—not the availability of students who are always in short supply, seemingly exactly when an educational researcher needs them the most.

So let's explore a sampling list of possible options for making those crucial interim decisions when faced with a proverbial fork in the road. As a disclaimer, however, please note that the following discussion does *not* refer to *efficacy* experiments involving the evaluation of a product against an *appropriate* control group. The rules and sample size requirements are well established for this type of research (Bausell 2015). Instead, the suggested options involve sequential development decisions that must sometimes be made along the way *prior* to the evaluation of a completed project. Decisions, in other words, for which investigators cannot afford to employ the relatively large sample sizes required by classic inferential statistical methods.

Why sequential studies often require impractically large sample sizes: As an example of this sample size problem, suppose a choice between two facets of an instructional product was necessary and the maximum learning difference that might be expected between them was "only" about one-half of a standard deviation (that is, an effect size or ES of 0.50). If the decision was to be based upon the results accruing from a simple two-group randomized experiment, then 128 students would be required to have an 80 percent chance of achieving statistical significance at or below 0.05.

Now, of course, a serious developmental team should be able to summon the resources to conduct such a study but, unlike an efficacy experiment, developmental work usually requires *multiple* sequential decisions (hence experiments), each dependent upon past results. This results in an ever-decelerating ES and a concomitantly ever-accelerating p-value.

To illustrate, while it might be quite reasonable to select a targeted ES of 0.50 (one-half of a standard deviation) for the first decisional fork in the road, suppose that difference was achieved with option A being significantly superior to option B at $p \leq .05$? (Of course this doesn't mean that A is without question superior to B, only that it "probably" is.)

But what if, after additional work, a new option C became available that the investigators had reason to believe would be superior to old option A? Would an ES of 0.50 now be reasonable? If so, this would suggest that option C was actually superior to old option B by a full standard deviation (that is, ES = 1.0, the 0.50 ES difference between A and B actually obtained *plus* the 0.50 difference between B and C). If C involved a relatively minor tweak to B, such a large effect would probably be unrealistic and almost certainly a smaller ES between A and C would be hypothesized than between A and B, perhaps half the size. So if an ES of 0.25 was hypothesized, the sample size would need to be increased more than three-and-a-half times that of the original A versus B study!

Now admittedly these ESs are arbitrary, but the bottom line is that sequential incremental improvements to an instructional product are *often* smaller as the developmental process continues toward completion, hence the hypothesized ESs become smaller and classic inferential statistics based upon p-values become less and less practical.

And if the team had access to a statistical consultant (which it should), his or her advice would most likely involve:

1. Relaxing the p-value (which would increase the error rate for the team's decision commensurate with the reduction),
2. Employing a one-tailed test (which would reduce the required sample size for a fixed ES but not commensurate with the increased ESs that would probably result here), and/or
3. Employing different statistical approaches (which normally do not result in dramatic increases in statistical power).

So what to do? Some additional conventional possibilities involve:

1. Employing a design randomizing pairs of carefully matched Ss (that is, matched on a variable highly correlated with the outcome variable). If such a variable can be found that correlates, say, 0.60 with the outcome, the sample size can be reduced by more than half (Bausell and Li, 2002). Relatedly, employing a crossover design of some sort is also a possibility although obviously different curricula must be used. However, either strategy may not provide an acceptable chance of obtaining the revered p-value of choice. But both would help.
2. Visualizing each pair of the previously suggested randomized matched pair just mentioned as a sort of ordinal single subject experiment provides

the opportunity for a quasi-replication strategy. Thus a total N of 12 (six pairs) can result in statistical significance if one option numerically outperforms the other for all six pairs in the same direction, no matter how weakly. Analogously, this is equivalent to flipping a coin six times and achieving the same result. If there is a good reason to predict that one option *should* be superior to the other, five pairs could be employed and would produce a one-tailed $p \leq .05$ if the direction of the effect was correctly hypothesized a priori.
3. Replication. If a similar difference in the same direction between the two options is found, then considerably more confidence can be had in the resulting decision.

Other tie-breaking options less dependent upon p-values and large sample sizes:

1. Assuming that some form of learning is employed as the outcome variable, it is always a good idea to include a planned follow-up retention test as an auxiliary outcome (a week or so lag or even a few days is fine) in head-to-head decisional contrasts. Perhaps option C will elicit superior retention compared to option A, which would make the direction to take a no-brainer. This is unlikely but possible since we don't know as much about retention as we do about original learning. We know even less about transfer, but it certainly wouldn't hurt to include a few transfer items in both the original and follow-up contrasts. (These items should be analyzed separately since they might "water down" the ES.)
2. Another potential tie-breaking strategy could involve collecting additional affective data to ascertain if one option is more palatable to students than another. This could be ascertained by the use of something as simple as an eleven-point visual analog scale anchored by one's choice of adjectives (terrible to great, boring to interesting, and so forth). Since this type of data can be so easily and quickly collected digitally, it is probably always wise to do so. If nothing else, building a database involving the same item(s) may be useful down the road for other decisions or even for the development of other products. (Naturally the scales themselves would need to be piloted.)
3. *Observation*! Old-fashioned perhaps—and hopefully not reminiscent of Lee J. Cronbach's (1975) regression—but we can learn a lot by simply observing people's behaviors and affect closely. If Ss are run individually, there is also no reason why each session can't be taped (especially for digital instruction since they will be sitting directly in front of a monitor) and viewed at a later time.

4. As a research *team*, much can be learned by retrospectively examining the results and the experimental procedures employed with an eye toward discovering some error, shortcomings, or hint in a study that may have influenced the results. Also revisiting the original rationale for contrasting the two options in the first place, using our working hypothesis and common sense, can help to explain why a preferred option was *not* as superior as expected. (A reconsideration of which option might be more acceptable to stakeholders other than students [for example, teachers, parents, administrators, critics] might also be undertaken.) True, all of this is hindsight, but hindsight is often correct and occasionally even helpful.
5. Setting a priori *minimum acceptable learning difference standards* is also a possibility, especially as investigators become more and more familiar with the instructional objectives being taught (for example, via pretest-posttest changes resulting from other pilot work). Thus if such an a priori criterion is achieved, perhaps it can be considered "good enough" for decisional purposes.
6. Sometimes one *component* or facet of two indistinguishable options may seem promising (for example, based upon observation or Ss' ratings). It may then be feasible to incorporate said component into the other intervention. Education is unique among the sciences in the sense that (a) it has a preeminently important outcome variable (learning) and (b) the effects of many of its interventions upon that outcome (learning) are *potentially cumulative* in nature.

In fact, one of the primary shortcomings of the science of education itself is the failure to recognize, document, and exploit this cumulative characteristic. The generic factorial design depicted in table 3.1 is an excellent way to assess whether such a cumulative effect occurs.

Table 3.1. A Two-Intervention 2 x 2 Factorial Design

	[B1] Receives Some Version of B	[B2] Receives No Version of B	Intervention A Contrast
[A1] Receives *Some* Version of A	[Cell A1B1] Both Intervention A & B (AB)	[Cell A1B2] Intervention A Only (A)	Mean (A1B1 + A1B2) [AB + A]
[A2] Receives *No* Version of A	[Cell A2B1] Intervention B Only (B)	[Cell A2B2] Neither A nor B (Control)	Mean (A2B1 + A2B2) [B + Control]
Intervention B Contrast	Mean (A1B1 + A2B1) (AB + B)	Mean (A1B2 + A2B2) (A + Control)	

This design is also an efficient way to eventually discover the elusive Holy Grail of educational research: synergistic effects (that is, A1B1 > [A1B2 − A2B2] + [A2B1 − A2B2]) if indeed such effects actually exist in our discipline).

7. Related to the possibility of cumulativeness (or synergism) and the complete freedom of developmental investigators to change directions in midstream, suppose a team comes to suspect that a product's true potential may reside in its auxiliary role with respect to another instructional modality (as the Ellson team did by [presumably] reconceptualizing the programmed tutoring product from a stand-alone intervention to an adjunct of classroom instruction). This freedom could take the form of adding *anything* (for example, a taped didactic to a digital lesson or any other type of presentation) related to a product's instructional objectives. These effects could be evaluated via a simple two-group design (the favored option up to that point versus that option + the other modality) or a version of the 2 × 2 design just suggested.

8. Assuming that instructional objectives have been employed (and this is always recommended), it is essential to examine the Ss' performance on each objective separately. (This should always be done anyway since it may hold the most important key to improving an instructional product.) True, some objectives and items are more difficult than others to evaluate but this will already be known via pretest-posttest pilot studies. In head-to-head comparisons, a substantive difference in performance on certain items may well inform which option should be used or how an option could be improved upon by adding a bit more instruction when performance on an objective is comparably poor. Or, given the freedom bequeathed to developmental investigators, the original instructional objectives (or even topic area) could be changed.

9. Increasing the number of objectives taught or the amount of instructional time employed might increase the ES. (Actually both options should probably be piloted prior to the beginning of the sequential process.)

10. But if none of this works (or isn't feasible), borrow a page from J. M. Stephens' (1967) relaxation principle and RELAX! Perhaps there is no reason to perseverate too compulsively over a directional decision. In the long run, an incorrect decision may not make all that much difference because there aren't too many differences in education that do matter all that much (except those involving more instruction or more relevant instruction). Or, since hindsight is always clearer than other views, if it becomes obvious later that a wrong fork in the road was taken, it is always possible to go back and explore the alternative route. After all,

product development in education is not a race. The important thing is to get it right.
11. And finally, if that advice is unsatisfactory there is always the possibility of appealing to authority, which is:

DOUG ELLSON'S APPROACH TO EVALUATING SEQUENTIAL EXPERIMENTS

Of all the examples of product-development work with which the present author is familiar, the Ellson programmed tutoring approach discussed in the first chapter may be the most informative since he left us a complete written record of his pilot work and his decisional processes. So, let's briefly review how the team of Ellson, Barber, Engle, and Kampwerth (1965) dealt with some of the issues just discussed.

It will be recalled that ten experiments were conducted (in addition to an unspecified amount of pilot work) to develop their programmed-tutoring product, some of which were sequential, some cumulative, and some neither. In a quick review of their experiments, it will be noted that they employed several of the non-probabilistically generated decisions listed above. Hardly coincidental, since the great man's approach informed many of these proffered strategies.

The first experiment involved thirty-eight individuals with a mean IQ of 54, the primary purpose being to ascertain if these individuals could be taught word recognition via the most mechanistic possible method and, if so, how much they would learn. The control was no instruction at all, which was as low a bar as they could devise, and a statistically significant p-value was correspondingly obtained. The second experiment involved ascertaining if similar effects could be obtained by employing "retarded" tutors. No inferential statistics at all were reported this time and none were really needed because this line of work was not pursued even though a large ES was obtained.

The third experiment tweaked the technique a bit, employed twelve Ss (same mean IQ), and again used a no-treatment control. It wasn't until the fourth experiment that programmed tutoring was compared to anything substantive and that one contrasted four groups of sixteen Ss, each involving:

1. Programmed tutoring alone,
2. Classroom instruction alone,
3. An alternation of the two, and
4. A no-treatment control.

(It could be argued that the latter group was not even necessary, but that is a matter of opinion. Plus, old habits and traditions are difficult [and sometimes unwise] to abandon.)

Statistical significance was found here for word recognition (both tutoring and the alternation of tutoring with classroom instruction) but not reading comprehension. However, no statistically significant differences were obtained between tutoring and the alternation of tutoring/classroom instruction with respect to either outcome, although there was a numerical trend for reading comprehension favoring the alternation group in comparison to classroom instruction alone. These results therefore highlight an important aspect of these investigators' developmental approach as illustrated at the juncture between their fourth and fifth experiments:

1. They had something that definitively worked for word recognition, but not reading comprehension: programmed tutoring alone or alternating with classroom instruction. However, no significant difference existed between the latter two.
2. They had produced a numerically (but not statistically) significant effect for programmed tutoring alternating with classroom instruction for reading comprehension.

So, what to do? From a conventional, one-study-and-done perspective, they would either have published their results or conducted a more definitive evaluation of their product prior to publishing it and then gone on to new (if not greener) pastures. After all, programmed tutoring worked for word recognition. So what if it didn't work better for reading comprehension?

However, from a developmental perspective, they were at an impasse. True, word recognition is a necessary condition for reading comprehension, but certainly not a sufficient one. In a sense, isn't the ability to comprehend what is read the more complete definition (and ultimate goal) of *reading instruction*?

Now, of course, the team's decision process is pure conjecture on the present author's part, but one option not chosen was to declare victory, publish their results, and then go on to something else. Another option would have been to tweak the reading-comprehension instruction and see if it could be demonstrated to be superior to classroom instruction. However, our investigators were encouraged by the finding that, even though alternating classroom instruction was not statistically superior to any of the other conditions with respect to reading comprehension, it was numerically superior to tutoring alone on both word recognition and reading comprehension.

Again, not having access to their thought processes, a safe guess is that our investigators *realized* that tutoring could never replace classroom instruction anyway so its adjunctive (or cumulative) effect became the objective of interest. And given the relatively minor word recognition difference between alternating the two and tutoring alone, a large-scale trial would have been needed to demonstrate a statistically significant difference between the two anyway. Also, the relatively more impressive *numerical* difference observed between the two interventions with respect to reading comprehension (the alternating-instruction mean was four times as great as the tutoring-alone mean) was probably quite heartening to the investigators because they knew (and transparently reported) that their Ss probably hadn't learned enough words in the sentences employed in this previous experiment to permit a reasonable degree of comprehension regarding those sentences.

They therefore had a theoretical (or commonsense) rationale for why the results for reading comprehension weren't as impressive as expected for alternating tutoring and classroom instruction, a policy reason for favoring alternation, and an encouraging numeric superiority for this option. All of these were reasonable bases for a decision as to which fork in the road to take.

So, the investigators may have made an executive decision based upon their product vision (that is, developmental objective) rather than Sir Ronald's suggested p-value and conducted their fifth experiment *without* programmed tutoring as a stand-alone intervention. They also tweaked their experimental design by *doubling* the amount of instruction employed to increase the ES (the ES, incidentally, has the most dramatic and effective method of increasing a study's statistical power, thereby reducing its required sample size).

And, given the realization that their intervention would undoubtedly be used in combination with classroom instruction in lieu of replacing it, they compared two *new* ways of combining programmed tutoring (their version of *cumulative research*) in addition to the promising alternating version employed in the fourth experiment (that is, tutoring following classroom instruction versus preceding it).

The gamble paid off and the alternating condition was superior to both of the new combinational methods, although statistical significance was obtained only for tutoring preceding classroom instruction. Heartened by this finding, the investigators went on to a completely different component of their programmed tutoring product: reinforcement schedules.

And that encapsulates one solution to sequential developmental research's problem of diminishing ESs as the product becomes more and more refined:

1. Leaning heavily upon *theory* (and perhaps even, heaven forbid, common sense),
2. Basing the developmental process on practical considerations involving how (and the environment in which) the product will be used,

3. Taking a *risk* when there is no obviously superior option, and finally, at the end of the journey,
4. Evaluating the final product via a carefully, fully powered, conventional randomized control trial.

And as we know, the fourth strategy was exemplarily accomplished in Ellson, Harris, and Barber's 1968 randomized evaluation (*A Field Test of Programed and Directed Tutoring*). Not only was the product significantly more effective than classroom instruction alone (which fifty years ago may not have been seen as tautological), it was more effective than tutoring designed by a reading expert as compared to their empirically developed form of tutoring involving a rigidly prescribed curriculum and procedural process.

All of this is, perhaps even unintentionally, more akin to the process employed in pure laboratory work involving rodents or bacteria by the more successful life sciences. True, these particular laboratory experiments can be mounted and replicated more quickly. Their "Ss" are also simpler to manipulate and more compliant, but educational researchers have chosen a different science, and if it is any consolation, our "laboratories" are usually *much* cheaper to set up and maintain (the Fuchs' work discussed in this book's companion volume being a notable exception).

And while perhaps not as comforting as a p-value, these proposed additions to our decision-making repertoire are not "unscientific," they simply aren't the way our profession is taught to conduct science—which surely isn't that big of a disadvantage given the discipline's track record. There is, after all, no guarantee that a single approach can guarantee the advancement of any science. The type of developmental research being advocated here is simply another option to the one-and-done-and-forgotten mentality that has characterized educational research for decades. In a nutshell, it involves the following process:

1. Constantly continuing to improve one's instructional interventions (or *inventions*) in order to improve student learning with an ultimate objective of improving, replacing, supplementing, or transforming the classic classroom,
2. Packaging one's best efforts in the form of a finished, implementable product,
3. Ensuring the marketing and/or disseminating of that product (otherwise it *won't* be implemented), *and*
4. Continuing all of the above by either extending the utility of the original product or beginning the development of a new one.

And while this genre of research may not be capable of transforming our science, hopefully its goal of *creating* the most effective learning products possible for any given educational setting, purpose, or group of objectives is worthy of some consideration by all educational scientists at some point during their (hopefully) long careers.

Chapter Four

Assessment Products that *Might* Contribute to a Useful Science of Education

Given the negative contributions made by classic psychometric research bequeathed to us by those misanthropic early intelligence test developers (as discussed in detail in this book's companion volume), some of the assessment products proposed in this chapter are made tentatively and with some misgivings. In defense of these proposals, however, none are based upon the normal curve, all measure *amount* rather than rank orders, and all would have already been developed in a more sensible science.

The last thing the science needs are more tests or scales based upon *any* psychometric model (be it classic measurement theory, item response theory, the Rasch model, ad nauseam) designed to assess intelligence, aptitude, motivation, personality, learning styles, inferred mental processes, or similarly bankrupt constructs. It may be helpful to place these contentious statements in context by restating four heretical principles, that is, four of the bogus assessment principles that were previously justified in the aforementioned companion volume:

1. *Ignore the items and you can call the test anything.* (The *items* are *what* is being measured.)
2. *Algebra can render otherwise noninterpretable test scores meaningful.*
3. *The stability (reliability) of a learning test is its most crucial characteristic and is a prerequisite for its utility.* Learning as a result of instruction is change.
4. *Writing a set of items to measure something, naming it, and correlating it with something else means (a) that the resulting instrument measures the construct its developer says it measures and (b) that the targeted construct exists*. This one encompasses just about every test, questionnaire, or inventory in psychology.

Also, as a general rule we don't need any more tests to predict future educational prognoses or behavior. We've been there, done that, and know the etiology of these criteria (be they the prediction of elementary school performance based upon tests administered prior to school entry, high school performance based upon tests administered in elementary school, college graduation based upon tests administered in high school, or later income based upon tests administered in college, noting the prestige of the college itself). We know that the regression coefficients linking anything vaguely cognitive with just about any other cognitive outcome will be statistically significant and we also know that most of these relationships reduce to self-fulfilling prophecies.

So perhaps we should award this one the status of an actual educational research principle (think the excrement and grandmother principles):

We don't need any more research involving the prediction of future performance, whether in terms of who will not succeed in college or become CEO of an investment banking firm.

Or for those who consider this one too negative, here is a more complimentary one:

To ascertain whether a child has the ability to learn a given topic, teach him/her and find out. To find out whether a teacher can teach, observe him/her. To improve instruction and thereby the amount learned, well, that's the purpose of product development research.

Everyone should have the opportunity to succeed with as much support as possible from the educational system and society as a whole and no one should be denied said opportunity based upon a test score. Tests exist to inform or improve instruction, *nothing more.* And yes, the present author does realize that less than 1 percent of the educational research community will agree with any of this but fortunately he is not writing this book seeking the acclaim or agreement of *anyone*. He is writing it to outline the infrastructure that is needed for his beloved science to evolve into something *useful*.

So with all of this said, it may be that there are a *few* openings for psychometrically inclined individuals to create a few auxiliary measures to facilitate this evolvement, *if* they are capable of reining in some of their baser predictive instincts—and if they are also willing to forego the use of *all* "mental," "psychological," "personality," and "predictive" measures along with constructs such as intelligence, central executive, processing speed, phonological loop, ad nauseam.

Naturally all of this may seem overly prescriptive and certainly it is meant to suggest a much-needed schism between psychology and education. However, psychology (*with the exception of educational psychology that deals with some facet of the curriculum, instruction, learning, or assessment of learning*) has little in common with education (and even less to contribute to it). In fact, psychology (like education) is itself a completely failed science so it is unlikely to contribute to the success of *anything*.

But perhaps your author is protesting too much, so let's simply review a few constructs that could be helpful for the digital-learning laboratory discussed in the previous chapter. And while the construction of the resulting measuring instruments would be greatly facilitated in a digital environment, they could be developed within even a traditional classroom setting.

BUT FIRST, A NECESSARY (OR AT LEAST PREFERABLE) PREREQUISITE PRODUCT: INSTRUCTIONAL OBJECTIVES

There are two reasons why our achievement tests are based upon the normal curve. One, as described in the companion volume, involved the unfortunate adoption by the intelligence test industry of the normal curve. This was an absolute necessity because while everyone thought they knew exactly what intelligence was, who had it, and certainly who didn't have it, no one knew how to test it.

In doing so, they made an absolutely incorrect assumption—namely, that intelligence was not amenable to instruction and hence was a stable trait. Accordingly, Alfred Binet, the developer of the most successful intelligence test, populated his measure with a smorgasbord of tasks that *weren't* normally part of the schooling curriculum—which if you think about it is a rather strange model to use for testing what *is* part of the curriculum.

But at least it is understandable *why* Binet and his successors relied on the normal curve to quantify their construct. Since they couldn't measure the *amount* of intelligence of any individual, they could use this rather impressive mathematical model to rank-order individual intelligence test *scores*, thereby estimating what proportion of scores (in a theoretically infinite population of humans) would be above or below any *individual*'s score on the test of interest.

And if you think about it, what other options would they have had? Of course now we know that intelligence tests do measure learning and vice versa (see Nisbett [2009] for an excellent, nontechnical review), but that is another story. What we also know is that the *amount* of learning can be quantified, however, based upon changes before and after instruction.

Constructing such a test is not an easy proposition, but it is possible if:

1. The curriculum is *exhaustively defined by instructional objectives* that can be addressed by single items,
2. These items, hence accompanying objectives, are rank-ordered with respect to difficulty level (which could be specified in terms of the average amount of instructional time each would require for mastery) and then sampled in some acceptable manner, and
3. Adaptive procedures are applied to avoid testing students on items that they are extremely likely to know.

To the extent that these conditions are met, the resulting scores can represent the proportion of the curriculum (whether for a grade level or some other unit) that the student has mastered. And this proportion, ranging from zero to one is a measure of *amount*.

The most immediate infrastructural prerequisite for this process involves *exhaustively defining the curriculum via instructional objectives*. This could be done for each subject-matter area for each grade, although it would probably be more useful if grade level was ignored and objectives for each topic were delineated from the most simple to a level of difficulty commensurate to, say, high school or college-level entry courses.

In the case of mathematics and literacy, the common core curriculum is already fairly well specified by agreed-upon standards, although most of these are too broad to be represented by one or two items. Breaking subject matter down into its smallest possible units (that is, instructional objectives or actual test items) is preferable from both the perspective of creating curricular products and testing.

The huge advantages of instructional objectives are their explicitness and the fact that they constitute the smallest possible units of instruction. In some cases, such as single-digit addition, it may be sufficient to write a single objective involving the addition of whole numbers ≤ 10.

Or, to use another example, while an educational *standard* such as "to learn exponential notation and perform elementary computations using it" may appear to be self-contained, it isn't *nearly* specific enough and actually constitutes myriad instructional objectives. However, few instructional topics are unconnected from their predecessors and successors in the curriculum and this one would not be very helpful to:

1. A teacher charged with its instruction,
2. A test developer charged with constructing a non-normed test on the subject, or
3. A curriculum developer working on a digital instructional unit on exponents.

All of these actors know how to personally solve a problem such as "$3^2 =$ ___," for example, but none may know all of the necessary components of the topic and some may have no concept of how to reformulate a problem such as "$3^2 \times 3^2 =$ ___," or that the process of doing so is encompassed in a broadly stated standard.

Now, granted, textbooks and instructional manuals exist for this purpose. However, something much more detailed and prescriptive is envisioned here, which is stated in behavioral, operational terms, such as:

Rename a number to the "zero power" as 1.

And to be maximally effective for both instructional and test construction purposes, it should be accompanied by sample items such as:

1. $3^0 =$ ___.
2. If $142^x = 1$, what is the exponent "x" equal to? ___

And perhaps buttressed (but not replaced) by multiple-choice items, if summative tests remained in that format (although there is no reason they should in a digital testing and scoring system) such as:

1. $3^0 =$ ___.
   a. 0
   b. 3
   c. 1
   d. 30
2. If $142^x = 1$, what is the exponent "x" equal to? ___
   a. 1
   b. 142
   c. 1/142
   d. 0

Similarly, explicit instructional objectives can be written for any subject matter at any level. With respect to introducing exponential notation and basic operations thereupon, more than a dozen or so such explicit objectives would need to be written (at least for younger students). Some objectives can potentially be mastered in a few minutes; some may take *much* longer (such as a reading objective that calls for sight recognition of the one hundred most employed words in children's literature, which it could be argued actually entails one hundred objectives, but let's not get overzealous here).

Constructing instructional objectives for topics like critical or creative thinking, and some educational goals, such as transfer of learning, would certainly be more difficult than others (and certainly more difficult to teach), but perhaps another educational research law may provide encouragement for anyone interested in going into this line of research:

Anything that can be learned can be taught, anything that can be taught can be tested, and instructional objectives can be written for anything that can be taught or tested.

Or its corollary:

Anything that can't be reduced to instructional objectives shouldn't be taught until it can be.

Of course, many different levels of complexity for different types of instructional objectives exist. Benjamin Bloom, whose instruction → learning work has been discussed with some reverence in the book's companion volume, actually had an unusual (perhaps unique) career in the sense that he is associated with two seminal achievements in two different areas of endeavor. Not only was he arguably the preeminent learning theorist and researcher of what might be described as the golden era of educational research (that is, 1970s and 1980s), he was also the lead editor of the first volume (the cognitive domain) of the landmark taxonomy of educational objectives (Bloom, Engelhart, Furst, et al., 1956). This Herculean project is one of the most-cited works in the field of education (more than 20,000 times and counting) and illustrative of the wide range of complexity that instructional objectives are capable of capturing (and that are capable of being taught).

It is the cognitive domain that is our concern here, whose superordinate categories (in order of complexity, and probably the amount of instructional time to master any attendant objectives based upon them) are:

1. Knowledge (broken into twelve subordinate categories)
2. Comprehension,
3. Application,
4. Analysis,
5. Synthesis, and
6. Evaluation.

A few decades later, Lorin Anderson (a student of Bloom's), David Krathwohl (one of the original editors of the taxonomy), and others published a revision (Anderson, Krathwohl, Airasian, et al., 2001) whose categories were not identical but somewhat similar, interfacing nicely with a briefer set of knowledge levels (that is, factual, conceptual, procedural, and metacognitive).

The Anderson and Krathwohl cognitive categories (also hierarchical in nature, and probably ordered based upon the amount of required time-on-task needed for mastery) were:

1. Remembering: which includes *recognizing* and *recalling*,
2. Understanding: *interpreting*, *exemplifying*, *classifying*, *summarizing*, *inferring*, *comparing*, and *explaining*,
3. Applying: involves *executing* and *implementing*, but appears to mean applying a procedure to either a familiar or unfamiliar task,
4. Analyzing: which involves *differentiating* and *organizing*, among other things,
5. Evaluating: which involves skills such as critical thinking, and
6. Creating: which involves *generating*, *planning*, *inventing*, and *producing* something.

So what's the product? "Little" more than a digitized and much-expanded version of another such product envisioned and begun decades ago by W. James Popham called the *instructional objectives exchange* (IOX). Popham's vision involved persuading elementary and secondary educators to pool their instructional objectives with the goal of covering the entire curriculum. The objectives themselves were visualized as facilitating both instruction and testing, while the primary focus here is upon (a) alternative instructional products (for example, digital, remote, and face-to-face tutoring) and (b) test construction designed to assess the amount learned rather than comparing students' test scores with one another.

There is no question that objectives can be somewhat irritating in their wordiness and stylized language conventions. Understandably, early works such as Bloom, et al. (1956) and Mager (1962) stressed the use of action verbs and other concise language conventions to ensure that educators, test constructors, and curriculum designers were clear about (and could communicate precisely) what was to be taught, learned, and tested.

However, there is no reason to be quite this doctrinaire. Perhaps prose objectives aren't even needed since our focus here is not on classroom instruction. Perhaps a group of items similar to those upon which students will be tested would be sufficient because if items are written for every facet of an instructional topic that needs to be learned, instructional products and tests designed to evaluate them would be greatly facilitated.

And there is one very large upside to the creation of this key infrastructural product. The vast majority of the necessary objectives already exist on the Internet or in textbooks (even older additions). It is "only" a matter of finding, editing, and categorizing them. It is also important to remember that, while creating such a product for an entire subject-matter K–12 curriculum may be quite daunting, there is no reason why it can't be developed on a piecemeal basis—product by product, instruction module by instruction module.

Regardless of how it is developed (full-blown or piecemeal) the product itself would be digital, searchable, and could be keyed to common core standards, commercial textbooks (many of which employ very explicit objectives themselves), and of course any test used to assess learning, achievement, mastery of the curriculum, or however its authors choose to label it.

Optimally too (although not absolutely essential), each objective could also contain a *brief* explanation regarding how it fits into the larger body of knowledge to which it belongs, which should itself facilitate the creation of an instructional product and might or might not be shared in a simpler form with students.

Thus returning to our simpleminded exponent objective (renaming a number to the "zero power" as 1), this digitally available mathematical explanation might take the following form:

> *By definition any whole number ≥ 0 raised to the zero power is equal to 1 (that is, $x^0 = 1$; $3^0 = 1$; $20^0 = 1$; and so forth). It is necessary to define it this way in order to be consistent with other definitions and properties involving exponents. As only one example, consider the objective in which students are expected to rename the product of two numbers with like bases as the common base with an exponent equal to the sum of the two exponents (that is, $x^4 * x^5 = x^{4+5} = x^9$). This means that $x^4 * x^0 = x^{4+0} = x^4$, which is consistent, since any number times 1 is equal to that number (that is, $2 * 1 = 1$ and $x^4 * 1 = x^4$). In mathematics, the operations and definitions used in one system of numbers (such as whole numbers) must be consistent with all of the others (such as exponents or rational numbers), otherwise mathematics itself would be inconsistent.*

A product such as this obviously can't be evaluated via p-values or hypothesis testing. It also can't be sold, but it is an infrastructural component that would greatly facilitate the development of other instructional products.

AVERAGE REQUIRED LEARNING TIME

In a previous book on school reform (Bausell, 2010) a scenario was presented in which a parent at a parent-teacher conference asked the teacher how long it would take her second-grade child (Samantha) to "catch up," given that she could read less than fifty words. The teacher, who didn't even know that much about Samantha's lack of reading progress because the school's reading achievement test was designed to provide information on Samantha's rank among all second graders, was at a complete loss as to how to answer the question. And the district's reading specialist was also in the same quandary, although this individual did suggest that a tutor be provided for Samantha (which was very excellent advice) although when queried how much tutoring would be required, the "expert" was again clueless.

And unfortunately so would we all be clueless, regardless of how many test scores might be available on the poor child. The best option, therefore, would be to simply tutor Samantha until she did "catch up." But wouldn't it be nice if we could affix an average amount of time required for key instructional objectives to be learned?

In a digital-instructional environment, this type of information could be collected automatically and this is the product envisioned here. (Such data could also be collected with more difficulty from face-to-face or remote tutoring.) Regardless of modality, the results could then be averaged across a given number of sessions along with ranges accompanying these averages since there would undoubtedly be individual differences in time required.

TOTAL OBJECTIVES LEARNED

This assessment project is not so much a construct as a statement of reality. It is also not tentatively proposed. It is a score that doesn't have to be stable (that is, reliable) and it doesn't have to be related to anything else (that is, valid) although, if it existed, it would surely generate a plethora of correlational studies. For want of a better term, let's just call this one *total objectives learned* (TOL).

As the name implies, this measure could indicate what proportion of the schooling curriculum any given student has mastered once the total curriculum (be it through a given grade level, the elementary school, middle school, high school, or the entire pre-K–12 schooling experience) has been transcribed into instructional objectives. It could also be expressed in terms of (or encompass only) certain subject matters, such as mathematics, reading, science, or topics thereof.

It could even encompass supplementary curricular objectives based upon modules developed by other professions and special interest groups if such a repository ever became available. Of course all of these resources, official and supplementary, would need to be carefully monitored for quality control purposes.

As mentioned previously, if instruction were to be digitalized in some manner, extremely comprehensive and detailed records could be kept for each student throughout the school year (or the entire schooling process for that matter) regarding which objectives had been mastered. (Hopefully this information would also be copied to a national database so that students' learning records would be available when they moved from school to school and from state to state.)

As an aside, consider what a different animal these records would be compared to those presently composed of a few standardized tests reported in terms of standardized scores (often with missing entries due to absences or clerical errors). Any student's teacher (whether the current one or the one to whom he or she had been assigned after moving from Mississippi to Oregon) could immediately ascertain what academic topics had been mastered and which ones needed to be learned. Or, in a truly digitalized model, a learning technologist (or someone with a presently nonexistent job description) could seamlessly plug the student into the new school's databased instructional sequence.

While a manned mission to Pluto is more likely to occur before such a system is realized, there is no reason why developmental work on a TOL measure (or simply a more comprehensive and universal minimum model student record system) could not be constructed, perhaps beginning with a single subject-matter topic.

This strategy has been briefly described with respect to the proposed digitally enhanced classroom, but the utility of assessing learning in this way should be pursued aggressively irrespective of instructional modality. In fact it should be used to eventually replace all norm-based achievement tests in use today, which would be a huge boon for educational research.

REQUIRED LEARNING TIME AS AN INDIVIDUAL CONSTRUCT

Given the preeminent importance of instructional time in our working hypothesis, one *potentially* useful measure for developmental research might involve a construct that, for want of a better term, could be called *individually required learning time* (IRLT). Given what we know (and often bemoan) about the huge individual differences in the amount of time required to learn just about every component of the school curriculum, isn't it odd that somewhere within the tens of thousands of educational and psychological assessments that have been developed we cannot measure these individual differences *directly*?

The construct itself is somewhat akin to the *response to intervention* concept, but the latter is primarily used to identify students who require an extra tier of instructional support. IRLT, on the other hand, could be used for this purpose plus two other functions.

First, it could quantify individual differences in the amount of time students require to learn certain standardized, ubiquitous instructional objectives (for example, an agreed-upon list of sight words). Second, it could eventually enable researchers to estimate how much remedial instruction time is required for individual ("at risk") students to "catch up" with their classmates on specific curricular topics.

Since learning speed is correlated with such constructs as intelligence (a type of learning), achievement (also a type of learning as measured by standardized commercial tests), SES, and all other things good and bright, then most likely IRLT would have the same etiology—the most important part of which (barring an organic condition or injury) is, for those readers not paying attention, the *amount of previous instruction received*. If this, our working hypothesis, is true, then IRLT is malleable and, like most components of human behavior, is subject to a practice effect. But how malleable this one is, we don't know.

There are many strategies by which a measure such as IRLT could be constructed, one of which might simply be the data eventually emanating from digital learning modules in which time and mastery would almost certainly be routinely collected electronically. Human (face-to-face and remote) tutoring would probably constitute the next best option since purposefully diverse groups of students could be employed. Alternately, standardized instructional objectives could be taught via classroom instruction to representative samples of students much in the way that achievement tests are calibrated, with time-to-mastery data collected on these samples.

Regardless of the instructional modality, it would be preferable for as many different sets of instructional objectives to be taught to the *same* students as possible, although this might be difficult, since no one in the calibrating efforts should have been taught any of the targeted objectives. However, without going into detail regarding how such a measure should be developed, let's explore some of the functions IRLT might serve.

Let's begin with two questions that have been partially answered by decades-old studies, but are sufficiently important to deserve replication within specific learning environments such as digital instruction.

1. Just how diverse are individual differences in IRLT?
2. How stable is IRLT across time for related subject matter?

The earliest and most definitive answers to these questions were probably supplied by Benjamin Bloom (the preeminent educational theorist [and perhaps educational researcher] of his era) and Lorin Anderson (one of his students who went on to have an exemplary career of his own).

Bloom (1974) estimated that some students learn the same material much faster than others (*perhaps requiring from one-fifth to one-sixth as much time*—an absolutely *enormous* discrepancy). He argued further, however, that this learning time was quite *malleable,* and indeed Anderson (1976) demonstrated that with practice, testing, and remedial tutoring, *the time needed to learn decreases quickly with repeated experiences*. In Anderson's words:

> *Two major conclusions can be derived from this study. First, the amount of necessary time-on-task-to-criterion can be altered by an effective teaching-learning strategy such as mastery learning. Second, a relatively heterogeneous group of students can become quite homogeneous in the amount of time-on-task they require to learn a particular learning task after mastering a series of preparatory tasks. This would imply that if equality of learning outcomes is a desired goal in certain instances in education, it can be achieved by designing learning situations that allow for inequalities in the characteristics that students bring to the learning situation. If, on the other hand, students are presented with a learning situation in which all are given an equal amount of elapsed time and instructional help, the results would be unequal learning outcomes.* (pp. 232–33)

The development of such a measure could serve the following purposes for product development efforts:

1. Individual differences in learning would be available from scores resulting from studies employing fixed instructional intervals (for example, thirty minutes followed by a test on the objectives taught). However, differences in IRLT would be available only from studies in which students' time to mastery was assessed.
2. Assuming the same Ss were run in multiple studies, once a reasonably sized database is generated (perhaps twenty-five pairs to start, to provide adequate power to detect an r of 0.50), the consistency of IRLT between two different sets of objectives could be calculated. If an r of 0.50 was obtained, the confidence intervals would be a bit on the wide side, but if replicated with a different sample, this would be an interesting finding. A considerably lower correlation would not necessarily doom the project since multiple studies could then be assigned to two *sets* of results and averaged—thereby increasing the reliability of each set and the correlation between them. Whether IRLT would prove useful would depend upon subsequent work involving the construct's correlation with learning (and more importantly the degree to which additional instruction is made available to students).

There are so many parameters to consider here that a prediction regarding the stability of IRLT (if indeed it has any) is tenuous at best.

Alternately, if Bloom and Anderson are correct, students' IRLTs will improve with experience and familiarity with a particular learning environment and/or instructional approach. From this perspective, the stability of the construct will be attenuated by practice, thus more important questions become:

1. If IRLT is malleable, to what extent can it be improved? And how? Are there specific skills that can be taught to increase IRLT?
2. What interventions, other than increased practice, can improve its acquisition curve?
3. Do different subject matters (for example, mathematics versus reading comprehension) differ with respect to IRLT, both from a between- and within-subject perspective?
4. If the latter (for example, if some students require less than average IRLT to learn mathematical concepts than language-arts skills and others the exact opposite), what are these differences related to? Prior instruction (for example, parental emphases), past failures and successes, or some other combination as yet undetermined?
5. Are there specific skills that can be taught to increase IRLT?
6. And most importantly of all, what are the implications of IRLT differences? More instruction on the subject requiring more learning time, certainly. But what about the subject-matter areas in which students require less time to learn? Should they be encouraged to concentrate on them (for example, by exposing them to more advanced instructional objectives in said area)?

Naturally, anyone interested in pursuing this line of work must be prepared to answer the dreaded "So what?" question since there should be no more "knowledge for knowledge's sake" foolishness. In other words, what educational implications do these differences in IRLT possess for instruction and learning? In the event they exist, are they large enough to matter one way or another?

Now, certainly, this line of research may prove to be a dead-end; and in a sense, it runs counter to one of the most important meritocratic implications of our working hypothesis if we add "learning speed" thereto:

If instruction is made equally and easily accessible to everyone 24/7, the unequal learning field due to prior instruction resulting from wealth, privilege, learning speed, *and home environments can be drastically reduced—although perhaps never eliminated without huge doses of extra instruction.*

So, if true, why even investigate whether some students require more instructional time than others? Why not just let the poor eat more cake (that is, study harder)?

While this may appear to be a rhetorical question, it isn't. If IRLT proves to be a semi-stable construct moderately predictive of the length of time required to learn new objectives, it could prove to be a useful addition to our developmental research toolkits. If nothing else, it would allow researchers in this field to describe their subjects in a more useful manner to aid other teams working on similar questions.

As an example, suppose one team (A) found that Intervention X reduced learning time by 15 percent for a given set of objectives. If team B wanted to build upon this finding in some way, knowing the average IRLT of the original study Ss might prove helpful, especially if the same information was collected on team B's sample. In other words, knowledge of different studies' average IRLTs might facilitate comparing research results more meaningfully than an ordinal standardized ES (since the former is expressed in terms of a ratio level of measurement rather than an ordinal one).

However, by far the most important questions regarding the construct revolve around how much it can be reduced (and when and whether it needs to be). Since most salutary human activities improve with practice, it would be very surprising if Bloom and Anderson were incorrect and this one didn't. Similarly, many attributes (think physical strength) continue to increase for years without intervention, and can continue to do so much longer in the presence of a proven intervention (think exercise).

Using this analogy, additional questions of interest become:

1. Can IRLT be reduced significantly over and above its natural history?
2. If it can, is there any clinical reason to do so? The answer probably depends upon the size of the preexisting differences accompanied by the construct's degree of malleability. If, for example, child A takes three times as long to learn common instructional objectives as child B, then A may simply not have enough time in childhood to make up the learning gap that will result without some sort of intensive intervention (probably a heavy dose of face-to-face or remote tutoring), depending upon the number of objectives so affected. However, if the IRLT gap is minimal, perhaps the problem can be manageable and ameliorated with extra instruction.
3. Are there additional advantages to reducing IRLT analogous to those accruing from exercise (which is useful throughout the lifespan, even though strength and endurance declines toward the end thereof)? Probably not, but it is an interesting question. Or, might students who take longer to learn something (and thus receive more instruction in the topic) retain

more of what they learned more slowly (and with greater effort) than their quicker counterparts? Or (hopefully not), might they forget it sooner? Again, probably neither, but we don't know. There is so very, very much we don't know about the seemingly simple Curriculum → Instruction → Learning ≈ Testing model.

4. If IRLT differs for students across subject-matter areas, does it predict subject-matter preference? In other words, do students prefer learning topics that they learn more quickly? If so, what is the causal mechanism—the chicken or the egg? Are there mediating variables, such as how early a topic is introduced (for example, via parental instruction [as always, broadly defined])? Or whether some teachers are more enthusiastic toward (or devote more instructional time to) the topic?

Now of course it is quite possible that the construct of IRLTs may well prove not to be stable or otherwise useful. But if so, nothing is lost except time if it is abandoned in a timely fashion. But now let's consider another potential component of individual differences in the time required for learning (if the construct exists) and a probable mediator of learning.

ENGAGEMENT WITH INSTRUCTION

Engagement has at least two aspects. One involves a student paying attention to instruction (as always broadly defined) and not daydreaming or engaging in disruptive behaviors in the classroom or tutoring session. The other is more closely associated with the verb (*to engage*) and is the one most in need of research since it requires students to voluntarily allocate more of their *time* to instruction.

Conceptually this latter version of the construct is related to motivation, but motivation is a nebulous mental process currently measured by self-report questionnaires, while engagement is a behavioral construct measured by how much *productive* time students are willing to (or capable of) devoting to learning. How useful such a measure would prove to be is unknown, but so are all of the other constructs suggested in this chapter.

Certainly engagement with digital instruction can and should be measured automatically, but the proportion of this time actively engaged with other instructional materials is a more challenging construct to measure. In digital instruction, proxy indicators such as keystrokes or scroll-downs can be recorded. "Wake-up messages" can also be issued to increase engagement, but the validity and utility of such strategies are not known and can undoubtedly be gamed. If digital engagement can be validity-assessed, it would open a tantalizing line of questions similar to IRLT, such as whether it is malleable, a crucial issue if digital instruction is ever freely available outside of school hours.

At present, the most commonly used nonobservational indicator we have of this genre of behavior in classroom instruction is student compliance with homework and other out-of-school assignments, which, like so many other factors, is largely a product of the home-learning environment. (Validity issues also exist, such as the possibility that someone other than the student completes the bulk of the assignments.)

In the classroom setting, engagement has been successfully measured by behavioral observations as witnessed by the *Beginning Teacher Evaluation* (Fisher, Berliner, Firby, et al., 1980) and *Instructional Dimensions Studies* previously (Cooley and Leinhardt, 1980) discussed in this book's companion volume.

Very promising work has also been conducted in a digital-learning environment as witnessed by a study performed by Beck (2005) in which the cloze procedure (that is, requiring students to fill in missing words) was used to ascertain the probability that a student was actively engaged in trying to answer questions in a digital-learning session. The author concluded that:

> Our model is sensitive enough to detect variations in student engagement within a single tutoring session. The novel aspect of this work is that it requires only data normally collected by a computer tutor, and the affective model [*note that the term "affective" does not indicate any sort of self-rating, but refers to speed and accuracy here in answering cloze items controlling for student ability and task difficulty*] is statistically validated against student performance on an external measure. (p. 88)

Obviously, a good deal of work remains to be done on this particular construct, so for the immediate future perhaps we should rely upon performance and observation when necessary. Or alternately, we could note the amount of time students voluntarily devote to working on a digital module or their compliance in making themselves available for digital tutoring sessions.

SUMMARY

A major step in the creation of the infrastructure needed for developing a clinically *useful* science of education would be taken if the three genres of data collection discussed in this chapter were completed. These are:

Assessment Products that Might Contribute to a Useful Science of Education 65

1. The translation of the curriculum into instructional objectives accompanied by the amount of instruction they require and learning tests based upon them,
2. The creation of the TOL (*total objectives learned*) formulation (which could be based upon individual topics, total grade-level standards, the entire public school curriculum, or anything in between), and
3. The IRLT (*individual required learning time*) construct (which would potentially be useful in decreasing disparities in school learning) could be used for at least two important functions.

This ends our discussion regarding the infrastructural components needed for both the development of viable digital products and the measurement products necessary to precisely assess the amount of learning achieved by students as opposed to their rank-ordering with one another on a hypothetical mathematical model. So it is now time to turn our attention to a number of products that might improve learning both within and as supplements to the much-maligned traditional classroom setting.

Chapter Five

Research that *Might* Improve Learning Despite the Traditional Classroom

As intractable as the classroom model is, there is little question that it *could* be improved. A great deal of research has been conducted to do just that, two of the most recent and well-publicized examples of which were discussed in this book's companion volume: the charter school initiative (which has a very strong theoretical and experimental basis via its extra instruction and tutoring) and the value-added teacher evaluation concept (which had no empirical basis and relied upon the proverbial "black box" as far as theory was concerned).

Let's therefore speculate how teacher *performance* might be manipulated to improve classroom learning. Now certainly this is a stretch but suppose a team of researchers decided to address some aspect of value-added teacher evaluation using our working hypothesis.

It's probably also too much to expect that present-day researchers would be familiar with such classic studies as the *Beginning Teacher Evaluation* (Fisher, Berliner, Firby, et al., 1980) or the *Instructional Dimensions* studies (Cooley and Leinhardt, 1980) discussed in this book's companion volume. But with respect to the etiology of teacher differences, the *Beginning Teacher Evaluation Study* investigators found that students of the top 10 percent of teachers received 71.4 days more instruction, or *a total of more than fourteen weeks of extra schooling*, than students of the bottom 10 percent of teachers.

That study itself should be sufficient to indicate how teaching could be made more effective. But since most educational scientists are not aware of decades-old research such as this, let's assume our hypothetical investigators decided to apply our more recently formulated working hypothesis to this most pressing of educational needs: the identification and amelioration of teachers whose students perform below expectations. Or perhaps a simple nudge from an extremely insightful *New York Times* Op Ed (Bausell, 2011) might serve the same purpose.

A CLASSROOM SURVEILLANCE SYSTEM

In response to one of these extremely unlikely events, suppose further that our backward-looking team began their work by posing the following questions:

Since we know the etiology of classroom learning and effective teaching, why wait for test results to arrive after the school year has been completed to find out which classrooms are and are not receiving their theoretically allocated dose of instruction?

And:

Why not also identify those classrooms unconducive to learning because insufficient instruction is being delivered and/or students are not attending to the instruction that is delivered due to the prevalence of adverse, competing stimuli (for example, noninstructional-related socialization, disruptive behaviors)?

Ergo:

Why not therefore position a few cheap cameras in each classroom to constantly pan the entire setting including students and teachers in order to identify teachers who are not delivering sufficient amounts of relevant instruction or who are experiencing difficulty in engaging students because of competing stimuli?

By:

Feeding the results into a central location (not necessarily within the school) where they are recorded, analyzed, and remediated in a timely manner?

Of course there are many diverse applications and iterations of the concept. For example, principals might appreciate the option of receiving real-time live feeds from each classroom. Teachers might also appreciate the ability to seamlessly notify the principal or vice principal when an unusual incident or serious behavioral problem occurs by sending them a live feed, or by simply marking the point thereon with the press of a button for later review or as evidence for disbelieving parents.

There is nothing particularly daunting about any of the technology involved, however, although there would undoubtedly be unexpected equipment, recording, and archiving issues to be solved. There would also be some special software needed, but this probably already exists in the security arena.

Ultimately, of course, the tapes would need to be evaluated, but this could be done using randomly selected brief intervals in order to initially assess compliance with perhaps only three variables consonant with the original statement of purpose and guiding theory:

1. What proportion of the sampled time was the teacher engaged in teaching the curriculum (which might be simply defined as the general subject-matter area, or more explicitly as the specific instructional objectives targeted, if this information were available) as opposed to noninstructional activities (for example, classroom management)?
2. What proportion of the students appeared to be attending to the instruction? And relatedly,
3. What was the incidence of actual disruptive behaviors (including bullying)?

A surveillance system such as this is an example of an educational product whose tweaking and improvement have the potential of eventually improving classroom instruction. Of course all new products are accompanied by unanticipated glitches, requiring the procedures, equipment, placement of the equipment, and all other components to be tweaked over time. The best analogy probably remains the stereotypical tech entrepreneurs working to incessantly develop and improve a software system or an app. Surely no one in their right minds would think that anyone could write the code on their first try and then go directly to market.

While this analogy is less than perfect (if for no other reason than that our garage- or basement-based entrepreneurs aren't faced with a roomful of students), the bottom line is that innovations of any sort need considerable developmental work preliminary to, concurrently with, and subsequent to their introduction into either the marketplace or the public schools.

These preliminary developmental phases tend to be underemphasized (if mentioned at all) in the training of educational researchers. By implication, their omission suggests to some that an intervention inspirationally materializes out of thin air (or as a result of reading an article or two) at which point all that is required is to conduct an RCT (randomized control trial) to evaluate its effectiveness. Many academics probably don't even consider the type of preliminary work that goes into developing an operating system, a search engine, or writing code for some new application as "real" science—maybe it isn't for some sciences—but these are the very types of activities *this* science desperately needs; it has no viable alternatives thereto.

While we may have no difficulty recognizing a team of PhDs working in a laboratory running experiment after experiment searching for, say, a catalyst to permit one small step in a chain leading to another (perhaps unpublishable) preliminary step as working in pursuit of science, many of the instructors in our field don't consider a comparable approach in developing an educational product to be science. However, there's nothing that can be done about these outdated opinions except to ignore them, so let's continue with our hypothetical project and assume that:

1. The hardware for the system functions reliably and a reasonably sized, troubled school (or school district) somewhere has allowed it to be installed.
2. All classroom instruction in one (or at most two) subjects has been taped for a few weeks and a previously unemployed or retired individual has been given the task of monitoring the process and trained in coding five-minute samples chosen randomly from each teacher's scheduled mathematics or reading lessons via software written especially for the purpose.
3. The interrater reliability of three aspects of classroom behavior (instructional time, student engagement, and disruptive student behavior) has been computed and all three variables appear to be reliably coded. (Note that reliability of observations can be increased by averaging more segments of behaviors, thus, if the reliability of a single five-minute session is inadequate but promising, then multiple five-minute sessions can be averaged until an acceptable level of consistency is reached. Note also that there is nothing magical about this five-minute length segment; it was chosen arbitrarily for illustrative purposes only.)

But why wait for the evaluation results? Developmental work such as this is different from traditional experimental research since nothing needs to be hidden (for example, the hypothesis, the existence and identity of intervention versus comparison groups) from participants or institutional staff. And it certainly isn't necessary to wait until the results are in to tweak the system.

For example, if the principal wishes to periodically monitor classrooms during the developmental process and observes untoward behavior (or lack of instruction) in one, then there is no reason why he or she should not intervene. If it becomes apparent that something doesn't work, it can be changed. If something was overlooked, it can be added. The objective is a working product, not a confound-free inference accompanied by a p-value.

So once the hardware functions reliably and instructional time and gross classroom behaviors can be coded reliably, a number of small-scale experiments might then be conducted in which the product or process (that is, the monitoring of teacher and student classroom behavior) is constantly tweaked—an approach more commonly associated with a quality-improvement process than hypothesis-driven educational research. And, of course, at some point, the entire system might be evaluated, although this could present difficulties using a randomized or quasi-experimental trial since the very introduction of the intervention (classroom cameras) might itself be excessively reactive.

Taking one additional step away from traditional, well-controlled trials, the team might employ a simple pre-observation interval → camera introduction → post-observation interval → continued observation design. The results could be graphed and inferential statistics could be computed if desired, but the bottom line would be to ascertain whether salutary changes in behavior did occur following the introduction of the cameras and if so, whether these changes persisted when students and teachers became accustomed to the presence of said cameras.

Many unanswered problems exist with this or any project, some anticipated, some not. A few of these unknowns might even be answered by previous research, or by interviewing investigators thereof since a great deal of classroom observational research has been conducted in the past.

One obvious problem with the presently proposed study revolves around the issue of validly recording instructional time involving seatwork, since teachers don't simply lecture in front of a class all day. Consequently, there will be times when teachers are apparently doing very little except sitting at their desks while their students may be profitably engaged in learning activities. In others, the teachers may be circulating around the room supervising student progress, helping struggling students, or delivering individual or small-group instruction.

These and many other issues would need to be worked out. (Seatwork, for example, might be evaluated based upon the percentage of the class that seemed to be doing something other than daydreaming, misbehaving, or clandestinely talking to peers.) However, during this ongoing developmental process, a plethora of important research questions will undoubtedly arise, such as:

1. What additional instructional factors can be coded reliably? To what extent can teachers' coverage of the mandated curriculum be assessed?
2. Can the *behaviors* of individual students (such as those achieving below expectations) be targeted efficiently in order to diagnose reasons for failure? Can daydreaming or otherwise inattentive students be brought back online in a nondisruptive fashion? Would showing students their own tapes facilitate more productive behaviors?
3. What effect would making the tapes available to parents have? What influence would making tapes of didactic instruction available for review, for remedial purposes, or for absentees have? (In this era of uploading

everything to the Internet, care must be taken to ensure that the tapes are used only locally and not transmitted by email or any other medium.)
4. Could single-class micro-lessons involving a discrete set of instructional objectives accompanied by brief pre- and posttests be used as a tool for teachers to diagnose their pedagogical strengths and weaknesses? Could exemplary lessons (based upon "expert" judgments and student gains) be used as benchmarks for this purpose? Would teachers who were given access to such tapes (and the time to review them) deliver the same lesson more effectively than teachers who were not?
5. To what extent are any of these parameters related to student achievement or value-added teacher evaluations (if the latter are still being conducted by the time this product is tested)? Could these parameters simply be substituted for test-based teacher evaluations? Could they be used as evidence for the basic invalidity of the latter (or as a separate indicator) for those teachers *consistently* "producing" low student test scores, but who nevertheless taught in a satisfactory manner based upon their taped instructional performance?
6. Do low-income urban schools have previously unidentifiable instructional contexts that differ substantively from higher-income suburban ones? Or do certain classroom configurations (for example, homogeneous versus heterogeneous grouping, or different levels of the latter) differ in some important, observable (and therefore correctable) manner?

Whether the answers to such questions (which as always are only a sampling of possibilities) would prove useful obviously isn't known. Whether or not any changes that might result in the classroom environment would increase learning or even prove to be a profitable line of research also isn't known. And of course, the product itself and its development might take a completely different form than envisioned here.

The purpose of presenting such research proposals is simply to suggest some lines of inquiry for scientists who prefer to work within the limitations endemic to the traditional classroom environment and thereby improve its effectiveness while still conducting meaningful, nonrepetitive, nonobvious science.

In truth it isn't even clear whether the classroom model can be improved. An educational research historian wouldn't be particularly optimistic, and would probably regale anyone who would listen with how impervious the classroom environment is to change. Such a person would remind his or her audience how technological advances have revolutionized society as a whole, while the classroom hasn't changed dramatically since parents dropped their youngest children off at school on horseback.

Many (perhaps most) schools of education faculty (including many if not most educational researchers based therein) will have a naturally tendency to avoid change and continue their presently futile pursuits independent of the technological innovations wrought by the Internet, smartphones, increased surveillance capacity, and social media that will eventually overwhelm and revolutionize the traditional classroom. Scientifically, the choice is between a *Groundhog Day*–like time loop involving the conduct of basically the same experiments over and over again, changing only the vocabulary and perhaps adding a comma or two (or a cultural anthropological approach similar to studying indigenous societies somewhere in the South Pacific), as opposed to a resolute, tenacious, interventionist approach more similar to that of medicine, engineering, or entrepreneurship.

There is no question which one is the more difficult path. There is also no question which one will eventually prevail, if not inside the profession, in spite of it.

By now it should be apparent that almost all meaningful instructional research of the future will involve technology of *some* sort. Of course the profession can continue business as usual and even conduct additional tutoring and small-group studies, but toward what end? Even the classroom surveillance system suggested just discussed involves technology, although about the lowest tech product imaginable (at least in terms of facilitating classroom instruction). Surely almost everything else will involve some form of digital instruction or digital testing and much of that will be Internet-based.

Since the Internet can be used to supplement traditional classroom instruction, let's now consider two such possibilities: one involving instruction and one involving testing (the latter's primary purpose, it will be remembered always, being to guide and target additional instruction).

REMOTE HUMAN TUTORING

Because of its logistic and manpower disadvantages, human tutoring has been primarily conceptualized as a supplement to classroom instruction, either from a within-school perspective (for example, by employing teacher aides or volunteers) or as an extra-school adjunct for parents who can afford it. From a logistic perspective, however, and despite being a multibillion-dollar industry, extra-school tutoring has a major disadvantage. Either the tutee must travel to the tutor (which in the case of younger students requires parental shuttling) or the tutor must travel to the tutee. Both involve difficult scheduling adjustments and time commitments that decrease the modality's feasibility for many families.

From the perspective of volunteers or actual school employees conducting in-school tutoring, another logistical disadvantage involves the additional instructional space required. Despite its inadequacies, classroom instruction is logistically and spatially quite efficient in the sense that twenty to thirty students can be instructed at the same time in the same room. However, even four or five tutoring sessions conducted in the same room result in distractions and noise pollution that add yet another impediment to within-school tutoring. Using the time-honored cafeteria for such purposes is problematic for the same reason.

Furthermore, if tutored students are pulled out of regularly scheduled classroom instruction, our working hypothesis would predict that the loss of classroom instruction during the tutoring interval would attenuate the overall effectiveness of the process, even though a net learning gain would still result. The true potential of tutoring to increase or remediate student learning therefore appears to reside in its use as an additional source of instruction occurring after schooling hours or during noninstructional school time (assuming appropriate space is provided).

Relatively recently, however, for-profit companies such as *tutor.com* have begun offering online tutoring services that theoretically are capable of capturing the advantages of tutoring without the most serious of its logistic disadvantages. Therefore as either a potential research environment or a marketable product, much of the technology needed for remote tutoring appears to already exist.

Historically and as illustrated in several meta-analyses (for example, Cohen, Kulik, and Kulik, 1982; Cook, Scruggs, Mastropieri, and Castro, 1985; Elbaum, Vaughn, Hughes, and Moody, 2000), as well as in the Fuchs' experimental work described in the companion volume, the most intensive efforts to solve the manpower and student-traveling disadvantages of tutoring has been the use of in-class peer tutors and adult volunteers. However, the true potential of remote tutoring resides in the supposition that there is no reason why the tutoring process need be restricted to the tutor and the tutee sharing the same space. Thus, following the lead of online tutoring services, why couldn't the tutoring process be structured so that it can be used as a mainstream supplementary, remedial, and/or research-instructional platform to classroom instruction?

After all, assuming the technological problems have been (or could be) ironed out, most of the mechanisms that make face-to-face tutoring so effective can be integrated into a remote version incorporating the following components:

1. Small, microphone-equipped cameras being available on both tutor and tutee computers or tablet-type devices to display each person's face,
2. Instructional materials from the tutor, as well as written, typed, or drawn responses from the tutee, are also displayed on the opposite device,
3. Test items designed to assess mastery/non-mastery of the session's instructional content, along with retention of past sessions, are seamlessly administered by the tutor and automatically machine scored, thereby permitting the tutor to provide immediate feedback on correct and incorrect answers with cursory explanations and instruction regarding the latter, and
4. All such data could be stored, automatically summarized, and made easily accessible to program administrators, tutors, school personnel (if applicable), students, and parents.

From an instructional perspective, the tutor would have complete control over what the tutee sees and naturally would have real-time access to anything the tutee types or writes, with split-screen capability to allow both faces to always be on display.

From the learner's perspective, answers to questions and feedback on performance would also be available in real time. Touch screens equipped with styluses would facilitate the process, giving both parties the capability of writing directly on their devices to display information on the other's screen. This could be used to physically communicate a correct response or to immediately cross out a mistake by supplying a cue or the correct response.

Naturally, such an arrangement would require developmental work, some involving software and some perhaps involving the adaptation of already existing hardware. Once perfected, however, besides its instructional value, this tutorial model could become a practical research platform as well as a medium for curriculum writers to design lessons (or translate textbook content) into remote tutoring lessons, keyed, as always, to either instructional objectives or the items reflecting the specific lesson content.

Of course a natural question becomes: who is going to adapt the technology just described? Probably not education faculty, although the hardware already exists—just not in an economically feasible form suitable for widespread implementation for the children who would profit most from it. And probably not Bill Gates, who understandably relies on advisors who seem to know nothing about the etiology of learning and instead prefer to waste his truly impressive generosity on dead-end educational initiatives, such as pushing value-added teacher evaluation without any consideration of the causative determinants of effective versus ineffective teachers. Nor would the IES redirect a major portion of its $200,000,000 budget to developing a product such as this when one researcher requires a total career funding just short of half that sum.

So while the answer to the question of *who* would develop such a system is not clear, the adaptation of cutting-edge technology to educational purposes is one of the ways that instructional time can be maximized and the science of education can be vitalized. With respect to the science, this *particular* product would also serve as an excellent instructional environment for any research team that preferred to conduct their studies free of the constraints inevitably accompanying work within the traditional classroom. Obviously one or more of the team members would require (or need to acquire) the necessary technological savvy, but this expertise already exists in the IT departments of some schools of education, and definitely *somewhere* within any research-intensive university.

The process could begin by (a) jury-rigging existing equipment (perhaps even discarded pieces in institutional IT graveyards), (b) starting from scratch with state-of-the art pieces of equipment, (c) beginning with an existing company's remote-tutoring platform and adapting it for research purposes, or (d) partnering with such a company.

Naturally, more than the requisite hardware and software would be required for the widespread implementation of remote tutoring to occur, including:

1. The transcription of the selected experimental curricula to explicitly communicable instructional units (again, objectives or simply sample items) accompanied by brief, quickly administrable learning assessments would need to be developed.
2. Explicit, scripted, programmatic tutoring units of perhaps thirty to forty minutes in duration would need to be developed based upon these objectives. (This is absolutely necessary because tutors should not be free to "do their own thing," thereby transferring the excrement principle from the classroom to the remote-tutoring process.)
3. Some resource by which economically disadvantaged students could be provided with the necessary resources (that is, the hardware, Internet connectivity, and technical support) would need to be identified. Libraries, community centers, and schools could be employed for these activities after hours, but individual, acoustically designed carrels would be necessary to ensure privacy and to decrease distractions. However, far and away the greatest potential for the location of this instruction would involve conducting the process within the home.
4. For the intervention to occur in the home, some accommodations must be made for economically depressed households. Perhaps used equipment could be donated by the private sector and adapted. Internet connectivity

might also be a problem, but perhaps some sort of limited-access system could be developed that permits communication only between limited sites, not conflicting with for-profit companies but actually provided thereby.
5. Storage, record keeping, and evaluation of identity-protected data on tutored students would need to be warehoused in an accessible manner somewhere.

And finally, most pressing of all, is the problem of obtaining tutors. At the risk of earning a naïveté diagnosis, perhaps some public-minded corporations could donate resources already available within their sphere of influence. Perhaps some could donate a small amount of employee time per week for free tutoring services to economically depressed families. Perhaps others could donate out-of-date computers, monitors, and servers that could be cannibalized to service the project. Or alternately, neighboring families with the requisite hardware could open their homes to a disadvantaged child for an hour or so a day in order to access the remote tutor.

While it is not possible to predict all of the applications that *could* emanate from a technological product such as this, the range of tutored curricula would probably be considerably greater than currently visualized and not limited to the school curriculum, basic academic subjects, or even students. Experts in myriad fields could offer tutorial services to adults, such as:

1. Statisticians providing personalized tutorials in the use of a specialized procedure or software application to funded researchers or their staffs,
2. Experienced interviewers and/or media specialists prepping applicants for impending job interviews (or experienced employees/experts in a field prepping job applicants on the basic knowledge needed for entry-level interviews in that field),
3. Sensitivity training for individuals about to be sent into other countries for sales or other business purposes,
4. Foreign language instruction, and
5. Tutoring in advanced computer, software, and Internet-search use.

More important to our purpose here than spawning a billion-dollar company or two, this product could constitute a renaissance for educational research. In addition to the developmental work required to make the medium more streamlined and learning effective, it would provide an incentive for creating the digital, curricular, and assessment resources that are needed for all types of instructional environments.

From a curricular perspective, just as instructional objectives should be written for each topic in the public school curriculum, scripted tutoring instruction (or at least detailed outlines thereof) should be prepared as well. Obviously deviations from these scripts would be necessitated based upon the individual requirements of the tutees, but pre-prepared lessons should be available to guide (and to a certain extent) standardize the content coverage.

None of the preceding suggestions are carved in stone and the developmental process may result in a completely different end-product than envisioned here. By its very nature, developmental research can take innumerable twists and turns requiring decisions—some minute in nature, some based upon informed guesses in the absence of data—that shape the final product in unanticipated, unintended ways.

Critics might argue that such a process is not science per se, but some combination of engineering and intuition, but again, so what? It is an example of the infrastructure this practice-oriented science needs to go alongside the specialized infrastructure this particular project requires (for example, instructional objectives, detailed lesson plans to facilitate their mastery, and a coordinating center of some sort). These latter three particular infrastructural components can and should be developed for any type of tutoring (face-to-face, remote, or digital) or instructional genre (for example, classroom or video).

While the creation of this sort of infrastructure may appear to be a daunting task, much of it already exists. Structured tutoring programs certainly do, some of which could hopefully be adapted for different purposes such as remote-tutoring or digital instruction. One of many examples is *Reading Rescue*, now a commercial product, developed decades ago by Marie Clay for struggling readers and shown to be more effective than no tutoring [duh] or small-group instruction [duh] for first-grade "language-minority" students (Ehri, Dreyer, Flugman, and Gross, 2007). Elementary mathematics tutoring manuals (*Pirate Math* and *Hot Math*) developed by Lynn Fuchs of Vanderbilt University provide another example.

The point is that a huge amount of curriculum development has already taken place specifically targeted to tutoring and even more can be adapted from other sources such as textbooks and workbooks. It's just a matter of finding it and perhaps tweaking it a bit because no one can patent or copyright the school curricula. And should anyone aspire to actually conduct research using the remote-tutoring paradigm, here is a very cursory sampling of the type of studies that might be conducted:

FACE-TO-FACE VERSUS REMOTE TUTORING

As a potential study, this one would appear to be a no-brainer since face-to-face tutoring would be expected to be slightly more effective than remote tutoring. However, it is difficult to predict the magnitude of the difference in terms of either additional learning or instructional time required for mastery of selected objectives. Until that metric is sufficiently developed, an observational study or two (or several) could be conducted to ascertain *why* face-to-face tutoring is superior to its remote counterpart when time, curriculum, student characteristics, and tutor differences are controlled. Not to provide an interesting answer to an interesting question or to generate knowledge for its own sake, but to potentially improve the *remote-tutoring* process.

These initial observational components (both modalities could be taped and analyzed later) could be examined to ascertain how the two methods differ with respect to key instructional variables such as (a) the number of questions asked by both tutors and tutees, (b) engagement by the tutee (a method for quantifying this construct would need to be developed, which is an area of research in and of itself), and (c) any other salient differences between the two. This is a line of work that definitely mandates the same tutors instructing matched pairs of tutees in both modalities (one tutee of the pair being randomly assigned to face-to-face tutoring with the other by default assigned to the remote option). A standardized script might also be indicated with the session tapes evaluated to ascertain fidelity thereto. (These procedures would allow a significantly reduced sample size while making the comparisons as sensitive as possible.)

Tutor training: The training of tutors could also be done remotely and should consist of at least one critiqued, videotaped, and face-to-face practice session conducted involving each unit taught (more would probably be necessary for a topic such as phonics instruction). Tutors should also be supplied with a list of the targeted objectives, sample items, and the rationale for why these objectives are important. (The latter should be shared with students in an age-appropriate manner.)

A single-page, large-font, checklist should also be provided to each tutor to be used for each lesson, which in turn would be composed of brief instructional units of probably no more than thirty-minutes' duration for younger students. Tutees would be pretested as part of the instructional session in order to personalize instruction. Posttesting might be repeated a day or two later to assess (and ensure) some degree of retention, but all of these strategies would be tested and altered if necessary as part of the developmental process.

Improvements to the process: Basically the developmental work would involve tweaking the instruction, the remote-tutoring process, and both the accompanying hardware and software. Since the objectives of this line of work are to (a) develop remote tutoring as a viable educational product and (b) continually improve it, the comparison group would probably involve the latest version of remote tutoring.

One of a multitude of examples of this type of research might involve optimizing the learning potential of the tests used to assess mastery of each session's content, such as:

1. What effect would the administration of the unit test have immediately prior to the tutoring session (or during it) upon learning and retention?
2. What constitutes optimal review (for example, timing, duration) of tutored content?
3. Could a module be revised in such a way that mastery of the objectives required less time?
4. Could an additional instructional objective or two be taught in the same time interval?

Dosage and duration issues must also be hammered out. Thirty to forty minutes appears to be an appropriate length for tutoring sessions involving young children but there aren't any controlled studies that test this limit. Thus more work is indicated to assess (a) whether longer or briefer sessions might prove profitable, (b) if computerized "homework" assignments should be added to the mix, (c) if a brief break in the middle of a session might facilitate learning, and/or (d) if tutee experience with the process increases tolerance and/or engagement (or has the opposite effect).

Transcription of remote tutoring to digital instruction (or vice versa): Since the tutoring sessions can be easily taped (and probably should be for quality assurance purposes), exemplary lessons could be used for (a) training purposes and (b) translation to digital-tutoring modules employing the same instructional objectives. Naturally a number of changes from the remote to the digital environment would be necessary, but remote-tutoring lessons could be used to jumpstart digital lessons or vice versa.

Tutor-to-tutee ratio: Could the remote tutoring model be tweaked to allow more than one tutee to be effectively taught by a single tutor during the same session? True, this is no longer tutoring, but given two students identified as having not mastered the same content, what would the learning costs be of a remote "tutor" simultaneously delivering the same lesson to both students housed at different locations from one another? Might there even be some benefits in interest or engagement levels? Could (and would) the same dyads work together cooperatively in the completion of computerized assignments?

Undoubtedly one-to-one tutoring would be more effective than small-group instruction, but the latter would be more efficient and remain more effective than classroom instruction. A previously mentioned, decades-old investigation (Moody, Bausell, and Jenkins, 1973) found that within a single class period, one-to-one human tutoring produced significantly more learning than one-to-two and one-to-five small-group instruction, but all were superior to classroom instruction. There is no reason why this finding would not also hold for remote tutoring, so perhaps there would be a future for "remote, small-group instruction" as long as everyone in the sessions needed instruction on the same objectives.

Developing the model solely for research purposes: There are procedural advantages to running Ss individually (for example, observing that the Ss are following the protocol and being able to redirect their efforts if their attention wavers) that must be weighed against the gains in efficiency occurring when they are run in groups. However, remotely running Ss in very small groups may capture the advantages of both strategies.

Employing the remote-tutoring model for running research Ss either individually or in groups of five or less may also facilitate the recruitment of Ss irrespective of geographic distance. It might even permit international recruitment and thereby greatly improve the generality of findings.

CURRICULUM-BASED MEASUREMENT FOR PARENTS

Curriculum-based measurement (CBM) was a strategy that became an actual movement, gaining a degree of traction in learning-disability and special-education circles. The late Stan Deno (1985) of the University of Minnesota was largely responsible for articulating the idea behind CBM and deserves much of the credit for its popularity.

CBM was originally conceived as a tool for allowing classroom teachers to "easily" and quickly administer extremely brief, readymade reading and math assessments throughout the school year. The purposes of these tests were to document individual learning progress throughout the year both (a) normatively (for example, by comparing each student's progress with his or her peers) and (b) individually (to ascertain what he or she had learned or failed to learn and thereby determine what he or she needed additional instruction upon).

This latter function, of course, is what assessment should involve but also what is patently impossible for commercial standardized tests to evaluate since they are typically administered at the end of the school year. Their results are therefore not available soon enough for remedial purposes nor are they specific or comprehensive enough to identify key objectives that students need extra instruction upon (even if there were some mechanism for delivery of said instruction).

The CBM concept was a commonsense, educationally brilliant innovation. It was especially apt for special-education and learning-disabled classroom environments because of their smaller size and their easier access to tutors. However, as brief and as simple as the CBM tests were, the strategy still required a good deal of effort on the part of teachers. Tests were not commonly administered digitally in the innovation's early years and other capabilities we now take for granted such as automatic machine scoring, storing, and graphing were not readily available.

Consequently the innovation never gained a great deal of traction in regular classrooms for several reasons, not the least of which were the difficulties of employing the strategy with twenty-five to thirty students. And while computers are more common in schools today, the software for CBM is not universally available, targeted instruction is often not feasible, and of course the excrement principle remains in full sway.

The product being suggested here differs very little from that original conception other than expanding its mini-tests to cover at least the entire elementary school math and reading curriculum (and definitely extending their use to all students, disadvantaged and not). However, to be maximally useful, CBM results would need to be available to parents as well as teachers and this would meet with a great deal of resistance in the present schooling system for obvious reasons. Realistically, then, the service would probably need to be offered by third parties *online* to allow parents to track their students' educational progress and to take action themselves if necessary.

Operationally the developmental process would entail collecting existing CBM assessments and creating new ones, placing them on a website searchable by subject matter and grade level, and making the tests available for parents to administer to their children at some fixed time interval (for example, monthly) in order to monitor their charges' actual *learning* progress over the course of the school year. There has been an enormous amount of research and developmental work already performed in this area (a good deal of it performed by both Professor Deno and the Fuchs teams' early work), so there would be no reason to reinvent the entire system—just enhance it.

Once developed, testing results might be displayed via simple two-line graphs depicting an individual student's progress versus the average of his or her peers to permit parents to ascertain the specific topics their children have and have not learned (as well as their progress thereon from the previous assessment). Since the purpose of *all* testing should be to guide instruction, optimally, tutoring lessons for supplemental parental instruction would be available for those willing and able to administer it. (In the best of worlds, these lessons would be digital in nature, but this might take a little time unless they were developed by the for-profit provider of the CBM system.)

Sharing these results with teachers would make parent-teacher conferences considerably more focused (and probably more confrontational unless the teacher had a preplanned course of action ready). However the best course of action for actual remediation in most cases would be for parents to either provide additional instruction at home or to seek help from a third-party tutoring service (that would be given the specific objectives upon which the students needed remediation).

READING FLUENCY AS AN EXAMPLE OF A CURRICULUM-BASED MEASUREMENT

One of the more interesting examples of CBM involves listening to a student read aloud from a previously unread grade-level text (defined as "challenging but manageable for the reader") for exactly one minute. A "words correct per minute" score is then derived by subtracting the number of words read incorrectly from the number read correctly. Hasbrouck and Tindal (2006) actually compiled a series of norms for various grade levels in a 1992 technical report, originally titled "Oral Reading Fluency: 90 Years of Measurement," that permitted a weekly gain in words correctly read from grades one through eight (see https://www.readnaturally.com/knowledgebase/how-to/9/59).

An important departure from traditional psychometric practice involved the norming of these assessments. They were not (and should not have been) based upon the normal curve, but rather represented the actual number of words read correctly and thus constituted a veridical measure of reading proficiency (as well as the *amount* of learning).

Obviously, with constantly improving voice-recognition capability, there is no reason why testing of this sort couldn't be computerized à la an adaptation of the previously discussed Automated Reading Tutor project. However CBM assessments can be so quickly administered and scored that most parents should be able to perform the necessary steps themselves without relying upon voice-recognition software.

Reading fluency and word recognition are among the easiest and most important assessments to administer since they involve little more than having children read a prose passages or a list of words. (Like just about everything else in education, reading fluency has been the subject of a meta-analysis [Yeo, 2008], in which the correlation between these one-minute assessments and reading *comprehension* was reported to be an astonishingly high 0.75.)

Accompanying instruction is equally painless, consisting of nothing more than reading to children, having them read appropriate passages (sometimes even what has been read to them), and teaching them words they have trouble with or are likely to encounter via flash cards.

This is only a sample of the types of nonprofit and for-profit educational products that should and could be developed to increase learning and access to instruction inside and outside of the traditional classroom. Next, let's consider a few potential products for the most important and impactful learning environment in existence. *Non-spoiler alert*: It isn't the traditional classroom.

Chapter Six

The Most Important Instructional Environment (and the Most Difficult to Improve)

The discrepancies between the amount of instruction received between children of different socioeconomic classes (and indeed within those designations) begins at least as early as age one and the gap continues to expand—picking up so much momentum that by age three the dye is set. And given the number of instructional hours this deficit can entail, there is no possible way that it can be made up within the traditional schooling paradigm.

Preventive childrearing education may be helpful, but it is not enough. And if manpower and economic constraints prohibit sufficient amounts of within-home tutoring (parental or remote) interventions, what is the answer? As always we have to look to digital instruction of some sort, but the form this instruction should take isn't obvious and requires some investigation.

Obviously a two-year-old can't be expected to (and shouldn't) sit at a computer or tablet and engage a virtual tutor even if these aides were available. And obviously parents in many households are too fatigued or stressed to begin teaching their toddlers academic content in any systematic way after a long work day, especially since many aren't sure what or how to do so. It can take a considerable amount of energy to sit down and try to teach a child academic content (especially in households with children of different ages with different academic needs).

But regardless of parental income, education, social status, or cultural background, all parents love their children equally and all want them to succeed. What they therefore need is the wherewithal to provide their children with effective but non-laborious academic instruction at least by the age of two.

The technology for doing this is available and being improved constantly, but much of it is priced outside of many families' budgets hence, from an equity standpoint, some version of it must be made accessible to all children.

At the time of this writing, there seems to be little possibility that these funds will come from the government, but philanthropic individuals and foundations could make a large dent in the educational disparities that begin so early in children's lives.

So let's envision two scenarios of what a parentally assisted two-year-old's education scenario might look like:

Scenario #1: The mother works for minimum wages at a hundred-billion-dollar retail mega-company in a job that requires her to be on her feet for eight hours. She takes the bus to pick up her two-year-old from a depressed daycare center and goes home to prepare dinner. While she does so, she is able to observe her child sitting in front of the television set, perhaps watching cartoons, perhaps an educational television show, perhaps old versions of *Pee-wee's Playhouse*.

After dinner and completely exhausted (she is pregnant with her second child) she wants nothing more than to sit down, watch television, play a few games with her child, some of which might even consist of trying to teach her letter names from a magazine she found on the bus, and then getting her to bed as soon as possible. During the weekend she gets to spend more time with her daughter and takes her to a local playground, perhaps visits friends, goes to church, and performs the multitude of tasks required in tending to an active two-year-old.

A couple of years later she enrolls her daughter in a preschool that employs no real instruction and claims to concentrate upon a few "readiness" activities, but otherwise resembles her daycare center more than a school, pre- or otherwise. The child therefore begins kindergarten without any substantive reading or math skills and performs near the median of her classes throughout the elementary years. Of course the median performance level of this inner city school's classroom is far below that of suburban schools only a few miles away.

After school the girl helps take care of her (now) two siblings and drops out of high school near the end of eleventh grade to work for a retail company similar to her mother's place of employment.

Scenario #2: This time, during her first pregnancy, the mother is bombarded with messages on bus billboards, television, and social media regarding the importance of talking to her baby constantly even if the infant doesn't appear to understand a word she is saying. When the child is one year of age, she is periodically provided with some appropriate storybooks by a volunteer who drops them off at her apartment and provides hints to both the child's mother and grandmother (who looks after her grandchild when her daughter is working) on how to read to the child (didactically and interactively by pointing to objects in the pictures).

At age two she is provided with a touch-screen tablet accompanied by limited Internet access sponsored by the Bill and Melinda Gates Foundation, which has come to realize that the billions spent on educational initiatives such as (a) value-added teacher evaluations that have no theoretical or practical rationale and (b) breaking up dysfunctional large schools into dysfunctional smaller ones were completely wasted.

The device itself is equipped with apps accessing modules containing letter names, numbers, shapes, colors, and common words typically employed in the storybooks she has been continually sent—also free of charge—and that her child has by then memorized.

Naturally the mother must work with the child on the tablet, but often she places her daughter with her back to the television while she herself watches it and provides feedback and encouragement at the same time. Or sometimes the daughter sits at the kitchen table and works on her device (or thumbs through one of the many books with which she has been supplied) while the mother multitasks as she prepares dinner and does other chores.

In a couple of years the mother is counseled by the volunteer (who still comes to her apartment once a month) to enroll her child in a somewhat less convenient but far more academically oriented pre-kindergarten class. Afterwards the mother applies for a slot in a nearby charter school, again at the recommendation of another volunteer who frequently communicates with her via email on her smartphone and who, through the same philanthropic organization, has secured Internet access for the family along with guidance regarding reading and math digital tutors available thereon.

The child performs consistently at the top of her class throughout the elementary school years (works with her two younger siblings on academic subjects a few hours each weekend) and does not drop out of school in eleventh grade. Instead she excels in a local community college and wins an academic scholarship to a prestigious state university where she declines membership to a "safe space" provided by politically active white female students: partly because she doesn't need one, partly because she isn't a white female student. And upon graduation, she also doesn't wind up being employed in a minimum-wage job, and neither do her children nor her grandchildren.

RESEARCH IMPLICATIONS

The development of the sort of infrastructure this vision requires is seldom considered scientific work, but it should be in education. It might seem important to evaluate whether infant educational initiatives such as these are effective, but we already know that if they are done correctly they will be—so why waste money on evaluation unless it is used for marketing purposes?

True, cajoling parents to change their rearing practices probably will have little effect without follow-up services such as just described, but they can be improved by the use of focus groups composed of members of the targeted audience. And we know that advertisement does work if the products are appealing and these will be, *if* they are accompanied by the promise of free counseling, free books, and free digital products.

The hardest task, therefore, will involve securing funding for such initiatives, many of which may be local in nature. But grant writing is even now considered part of science and so should this genre of research be, although certainly not as lucrative for the university (which shouldn't expect 50 percent or so of the award as "overhead" nor should the "investigators" expect to cover large swaths of their salaries therefrom).

However, such programs could generate a number of important research opportunities such as investigating:

1. The types of beginning books most popular with parents and their children (as reported by the parents).
2. Improvements in any of the instructional software designed to run on the donated tablets of other devices.
3. Whether a touch-screen cell phone (which almost everyone has regardless of their socioeconomic status) could serve in lieu of a tablet.
4. The optimal curricular progression for reading and math instruction.
5. After the letter names and a given number of words can be read by sight, which letter sounds and other phonetic content can be taught effectively (and how can they best be effectively be taught in this particular environment)?
6. Similarly, after basic numeration recognition and counting has been mastered, which other mathematical topics can be taught (and how should they be taught)?
7. Could some usage of this technologically enhanced early instruction be implemented in daycare centers, community centers, libraries, and so forth?

The children who have had access to these interventions could be followed longitudinally for (a) quality improvement purposes and (b) to attempt to ascertain what determines their optimal utilization, less-than-optimal utilization, and non-utilization, not necessarily to evaluate the effectiveness of the program, but in an attempt to identify preventable barriers to utilization.

At some point a longitudinal follow-up of a sample of children who have had access to these interventions might also be conducted to determine their future educational and employment outcomes. Again, this would be of interest not so much to evaluate the effectiveness of the program but to ascertain what effects the intervention (and the resulting learning therefrom) has upon children's futures.

A plethora of preschool and early childhood research has identified the most important determinant of children's classroom success as residing in what they bring with them when they first walk through the schoolhouse door, even more than what happens to them in the classroom. This finding was initially given credence by the most influential study ever conducted aptly titled the *Equality of Educational Opportunity* (but more commonly, referred to as simply the "Coleman Report" [1966]), with an equivalent conclusion being arrived at empirically over a decade earlier (see Kemp, 1955).

However, what neither of these seminal reports mentioned was the rather obvious implications that increased instruction taking place prior to school entry (and primarily administered within the home) has upon *school* and teacher *performance*. So let's award this implication the status of an *educational research principle*:

One of the most effective ways to increase learning within the classroom paradigm (and therefore improve individual schools and teacher performance) is to increase the amount of instruction administered within the home.

In other words, if more children could arrive at school with at least rudimentary reading, mathematical, and writing skills, schools could use the finite instructional time available to them far more efficiently and effectively—especially if surveillance systems were in place to monitor said instruction. This would not only reduce socioeconomic learning disparities among students but it would also greatly reduce differences in school performance due to the socioeconomic statuses of the populations schools serve.

So this is why the present chapter is titled "The Most Important Instructional Environment," the justification of which is supported by a plethora of early development and preschool research that constitutes one of the prime determinants of our working hypothesis—research results that are as obvious as our science itself.

This research has been reviewed in this book's accompanying volume as well as many, many other places, but the most important single study was undoubtedly conducted by Betty Hart and Todd Risley (1995) in which intensive in-home observations were conducted of children for two-and-a-half years beginning when they were one year old. The forty-two families represented diverse socioeconomic backgrounds and the findings were absolutely mind-bending.

The authors of this seminal study from our discipline's past left us a message that is so very relevant to our purposes here that it will be repeated in this book as well:

> intervening in the lives of children from families in poverty is considerably more complex than we thought, simply because the first 3 years of experience are so much more important than we thought. (p. 168)

But intervene the science of education *must* if the socioeconomic discrepancies in school success and later employment opportunities are to ever be ameliorated. And unfortunately it is not exactly clear, and certainly not to the present author given his limited gifts, how the societal will to do this can be summoned. Behavioral change, especially in child-rearing, is an exceedingly intractable variable and education designed to change such behaviors has never been particularly effective. (It may be a necessary condition perhaps, but certainly not a sufficient one.)

Highly educated parents not only talk to their children more (which is an important form of instruction) but they actively teach their children to recognized letters, words, numeration, and even how to read, count, and manipulate numbers before they enter school. Many less-educated parents in low-income households do not (or do so to a much lesser degree) and (in either an ordinal normal curve-based assessment system or an objective mastery-based one) their children have no chance to make up the resulting learning deficit without intensive interventions.

Part of this discrepancy may simply be the fact that lower socioeconomic status (SES) parents were not taught when they were children by their parents. Part may be that they received a substandard education in school and don't value education because it didn't do much for them.

Other reasons why educating such families is insufficient resides in systemic reasons why such intensive instruction is not administered within *their* homes, but the bottom line remains the same. Cajoling such parents regarding the importance of teaching their children academic skills at an early age or about the existence of educational television programs may be helpful, but it is not nearly enough to compensate for the lack of intensive parental tutoring that their children's peers from higher income families receive.

To some extent, technological-based interventions or products might be helpful here. And while Internet-connected computers may not be available in all low-income homes, almost everyone has a smartphone today and *all* children are fascinated by their parents' fascination therewith by the end of the first year of life. Almost everyone also has a television set, many of which are connected to the Internet, so access to instruction within the home is greater than the supply of such instruction itself.

Regardless of the specific avenues available, what more important infrastructural component for education and the development of a relevant education science could there be than making reading and math instruction available to all families 24/7? Couldn't a developmental team or group of teams partner with a corporation somewhere to come up with a robust "play" phone designed for nothing more than receiving such instruction? Perhaps just the lure of children having their own phones might be sufficiently motivating for many of them to engage in learning activities while their parents compulsively thumb through theirs.

CONCLUDING THOUGHTS

Besides the organization needed for initiatives such as these, all of them also require additional volunteers, whether in person or remote. Where all these individuals will come from is not known, but some options might be:

1. Students in the school of education could be required to devote three or four course credits' worth of effort to tutoring very young children,
2. Perhaps civic-minded corporations could donate a few hours of their employees' time to such activities, along with
3. A potpourri of other groups such as church members, retired individuals, high school students fulfilling public service requirements, and so forth.
4. Perhaps childcare providers could be required to engage in a minimum number of hours of academic instruction as a requirement of certification or licensing.

Obviously the present author doesn't have a definitive answer for how to engage society in this type of crucial, essential, early instruction—crucial *and* essential because if a huge amount of additional intensive instruction is not delivered to children who are not taught prior to arriving at school, it will not be possible for the deficit to be closed by school-based instruction. And this deficit is the primary engine driving the ever-widening socioeconomic gap afflicting this country, which should surely be a (or perhaps *the*) primary concern of an actual *science* of education.

Chapter Seven

Curriculum Research/Change

Of the four components of our Curriculum → Instruction → Learning ≈ Testing model, the curriculum is by far the most controversial and politically charged. For that reason curricular *changes* or *reforms* are especially fraught with difficulties. Some controversies are understandable given diverse religious and social orientations. Some much less so, such as the attitude that: "It may be boring and useless, but I had to learn it and it didn't hurt me!" (Of course it may have in the long run but that's another issue.)

So far, all the research examples presented in both this book and its companion volume have involved some aspect of instruction, learning, or testing in which the curriculum is assumed to be appropriate and hence has held constant while one or more of these three components is investigated. However, if *what* is taught or learned is worthless (à la the lyrics of the Paul Simon song), what does it matter how it is taught, how much of it is learned, or how it is tested?

Curriculum research, especially research involving curriculum *change*, is procedurally difficult to evaluate using learning as an outcome because if two different curricula (or different instructional objectives) are taught, students will naturally learn more of the curriculum that is taught (or emphasized more) and less of the curriculum that is taught less (or de-emphasized). So how does one evaluate the appropriateness of a curriculum or a curricular change?

Unfortunately the present author, like most other people, is more adept at posing questions than answering them. So the best answer to this one is "probably you can't" and questions involving "appropriateness" immediately lead to others such as "appropriateness with respect to what?" None of the answers proposed for such questions are especially amenable to arbitration via p-values.

Suffice it to say, then, that this chapter is destined to be a bit more theoretical than its predecessors and much more permissive with regard to its conception of what constitutes legitimate educational research. More specifically, no distinction is made between curriculum *research* and curriculum *change* (for instance, of the two examples of this genre of research or change [depending upon one's linguistic preferences] discussed, one was formally evaluated and one was not—but both were equally exceedingly ambitious undertakings).

Before considering some of the issues involved in this type of inquiry, however, it is important to acknowledge a distinction as well as a confusing relationship that have been ignored up to this point regarding our simplistic Curriculum → Instruction → Learning ≈ Testing model of what comprises the science of education.

First, there are two curriculums. One is the "official" curriculum that is what society (which might be represented by a single school district, state, or the nation as a whole) has decried *should* be taught (via standards, core objectives, or whatever). The other is the "operational" curriculum that is composed of what is actually *taught* based upon the instruction and instructional products to which students are exposed.

This may appear to be a trivial distinction and hopefully in most cases it is. However, while almost all teachers generally adhere to the "official curriculum," some:

1. May not be completely aware of everything contained therein that they are charged with teaching,
2. May make executive decisions regarding what is and is not appropriate for their students,
3. May deliver incorrect information, and/or
4. May choose to add some content that they feel students should learn even though it is not part of the "official" curriculum.

All of these deviations therefore comprise an "unofficial" or "incidental" curriculum, as do many instructional products such as textbooks or educational videos that are not necessarily tailored to a specific locale's "official" curriculum. For this chapter's purposes, therefore, it should always be assumed that we are dealing with the latter, however defined (and however inadequately it is done).

Of course the school curriculum is hardly a monolithic entity, but rather is composed (in the elementary grades alone) of very disparate:

1. Subject matters (for example, reading, mathematics, science, writing, and social studies),
2. Topic areas within subject matters (for example, within reading: word recognition, phonics, reading fluency, comprehension of what is read), and
3. Very specific instructional objectives (or similar breakdowns of "small bits" of instruction) within topic areas (for example, learning 90 percent of the sight words on various word lists, sounding out selected constant blends, and so forth).

In the best of possible educational worlds, curriculum evaluation (or review) would be a constant national exercise in which experts (or advocates) review topics and objectives from several different perspectives, including what should be deleted or added from the various school curricula at different grade levels. However (*spoiler alert*) the United States does not comprise the best of educational worlds and doesn't even have a national curriculum per se. But sometimes it's worth exploring what *should be* rather than what's likely to actually happen.

CURRICULUM REVIEW

Practically all educational research (indeed research in most disciplines) is conducted by teams of investigators rather than individuals working alone. Curriculum review, research, change, or evaluation (all are pretty much synonymous, so let's employ the former) definitely requires a dedicated team of individuals interacting with an even larger group who are also willing to share their expertise regarding what should be taught.

Later in the chapter, two seminal examples of the curricular change process will be discussed, one involving a philosophy of education and one involving a specific subject matter (mathematics) primarily driven by mathematicians. Both involved large committees of individuals willing to dedicate their time to the process and both involved strong leadership.

Before considering those examples and the lessons they have left us, let's explore the possibility of a more-focused endeavor that a team of curriculum specialists might undertake, perhaps by biting off a small piece of the curriculum and piloting an evaluation, convening a sample of online "experts" to drive the process.

Recalling the three tiers of the curriculum itself (subject matters, topics, and instructional objectives), a truly nationally based, ongoing curriculum review would periodically evaluate each topic area (subject matters are probably sacrosanct and therefore immune to considerations) based upon a review of the instructional objectives comprising it on several levels. The ultimate purpose of which (from the topic area's perspective) would be the following meta-issues:

1. Should the topic be retained or eliminated?
2. Should more or less emphasis (that is, instructional time) be devoted thereto?

Each instructional objective would be evaluated for the same reasons but the rationale for each objective's inclusion, exclusion, or change of emphasis would rest upon the responses to the following questions:

1. To what other instructional objective or topic is the mastery of this objective a prerequisite? From a curriculum review perspective, this question should be answered based upon a logical analysis of obviously superordinate, related objectives. It can also be answered empirically by teaching a superordinate objective (or set thereof) to students who have not yet mastered the supposed prerequisites.
2. Does it have any utility for future job, civic, social, or evolutionary/familial functioning? Most instructional objectives will be too specific and short-ranged to have such a grandiose purpose, but it is a question worth considering in the event that such an outcome constitutes the major rationale for teaching an objective.
3. Should (or could) it be taught later or earlier? Jerome Bruner (1960) once hypothesized (based upon a curriculum reform meeting sponsored by the National Academy of Sciences and the National Science Foundation) that any subject *could* be taught effectively to any child in an intellectually honest way at any stage of development, but whether this is true or not, the question remains "when *should* it be taught?"
4. To what other topics or skills is it hypothesized to transfer? As always, transfer is a particularly difficult construct to operationalize, so perhaps the best approach is to conduct a logical content analysis of the instructional objectives supporting any topic with an eye toward finding redundancies.
5. Are the advantages of learning the topic commensurate with the amount of instructional time required? This applies to all of the preceding rationales for teaching a topic. Unfortunately without access to the proposed required-learning-time database, judgments regarding this construct will have to be based upon gross estimates.

(Note that aesthetic, artistic, or quality benefits are not included here since these criteria are far above the present author's pay grade but there is no reason for a better-informed research team not to include them.)

LOCATING AND DELETING IRRELEVANCIES FROM THE CURRICULUM

For many topics and objectives, the preceding questions are quite difficult to address, so let's consider how two topics might be deleted from the curriculum based upon vernacular logic. This approach could be effectively employed by either a single individual or a team (in fact a team could be constituted to trawl the curriculum in search of irrelevancies and then construct a case for their deletion).

Given our focus on instructional time as education's most precious and finite resource, it is ridiculous that every topic in the curriculum isn't examined from a logical-behavioral perspective to ascertain if it could be deleted. The advantage of curricular deletion is obvious since fewer topics would potentially free up additional instructional time for more useful ones (that is, new ones or content currently being taught with less-than-perfect success).

To a certain extent, a few topics are very gradually dropped from the curriculum. Our first example involves one that appears to be the process of being relegated to the recycle bin.

CURSIVE WRITING

Cursive writing as an academic skill has been under siege for some time. It was part of the curriculum for almost everyone in previous generations, but only a very, very small minority of anyone born after the invention of instant messaging or email ever uses the skill. And certainly no one in the age of Facebook, Twitter, and Instagram will ever need to.

Even those adults who were laboriously taught cursive writing once they had been introduced to printing via the use of pencils (that is, an obsolete writing instrument for those below the age of twenty-five) may no longer use the skill. This is partly because their cursive calligraphy has degenerated over time, making it difficult to read; when anyone does communicate via handwritten format these days, they often choose to print since neither their audiences nor they themselves can read their cursive scribbling.

So why devote precious instructional time to teach it in the public schools? There are two reasons, neither of them sensible: cursive writing (a) has been taught in school for more than a century, and (b) it has passionate defenders—which leads to another dreaded digression, a curriculum research principle, and a strategy for dealing with it:

First, the digression: As many educational writers have lamented, just about everyone who has attended school considers himself or herself an expert on schooling. They know what schools look like and they remember *what* was taught, even if they've forgotten the specifics and would fail a test on the subject matter if tested today. Most parents want at least some version of what they remember receiving to be taught to their own children, which by definition includes being taught what they were taught, along with a very limited number of new topics; otherwise they fear their children are being shortchanged. Thus, the public is more amenable to adding *academic* topics to the curriculum than to deleting them. Teachers are generally resistive to changing the curriculum as well (with either additions or deletions) because (a) it makes their jobs more difficult and (b) they also went to school once too.

> *Now the law or principle:*
> One of the possessions humans hold onto most dearly (and find most difficult to relinquish) is what they've been taught and especially what they've learned (which of course is a lot less than [and may actually differ from] what they've been taught).

That's why education faculty, as well as those who teach research methods, will disagree with almost everything said so far and will be enraged by blasphemies such as the suggestion that the education they provide future teachers is a step down from worthless, or that the sacrosanct effect size is an ordinal statistic and does *not* represent the size of an effect.

> *And finally, the strategy for curriculum researchers to deal with both:*
> Explain the rationale for deletion patiently, clearly, and respectfully, and then ignore everyone's protestations.

Armed with this principle and its attendant strategy, let's briefly consider another example of irrelevant curricular content that does not appear to be on the way out. (There are, of course, many, many others.)

FRACTIONS

Few topics in the elementary school math curriculum involve more instructional time than computational operations involving fractions. It is also a safe bet that if elementary school teachers were queried regarding the most difficult content to teach, this one would wind up very near the top of the list. Most people not familiar with the elementary school curriculum would also be shocked at the inordinate amount of instructional time expended teaching children how to add, subtract, multiply, and divide fractions, not to mention converting them back and forth from "improper fractions" to "mixed numbers" and other machinations. But as predicted by our most recent principle, very few of these same people would ever question the need for such instruction—primarily because we aren't accustomed to questioning what our children are taught, as long as we were taught the same thing.

However, curriculum researchers' *first* inclination *should* be to question everything taught in school, and perhaps the first question (followed by some of the more specific criteria posed a little earlier) they should ask about every topic in the curriculum is:

What function does topic X serve in people's everyday societal functioning?

The primary function of fractions is linguistically oriented, such as in answer to the following question posed at the deli counter: "How much pastrami do you want?"

In which case, the answer is expected (and almost always provided) in terms of a fraction: "Oh, give me *about* a quarter of a pound."

And that's *about* all the utility there is for this particular notation system. True, the answer to such a question might be in terms of a mixed number: "Give me two and one-half pounds," but the deli employee is never going to ask you:

"Could you please convert that to an improper fraction [that is, 5/2] for me?"

And for most answers to queries regarding potential amounts of a whole, percentages are preferable such as: "How many people do you expect at our class reunion?"

"I doubt if more than 25 or 30 percent actually show up."

Even though it is a curricular staple, a case could be made that there is no known reason why an elementary school child should *ever* be taught to add, subtract, multiply, or divide fractions. For the majority of the present author's adult life in which he made his living working with numbers, the last time he was ever faced with a problem such as the following was in elementary school:

$14 \frac{1}{2} \div 17 \frac{3}{4} = \underline{\quad}$

And is it any wonder children experience difficulty learning (and retaining) such a computationally intensive and basically meaningless topic, or that it consumes so much instructional time?

In real-life computations, we use decimals (and occasionally percentages), not fractions. True, we use language that implies a fractional representation for example, "LeBron James has hit twenty-five of his last twenty-seven free throws"), but it's either percentages or decimal representations that are used to explicate them ("That comes out to making 93 percent of his free throws, which is third in the league.") If the announcer had reported that LeBron had made 25/27ths of his free throws, he or she might have been fired.

So that is probably the type of an initial, informal analysis than a curriculum research team might conduct before going on to consider other functions that fractions play in people's everyday societal functioning. And if they did so, the conclusion would probably be to teach students the (a) names of the most commonly used simple fractions in everyday communication (for example, halves, thirds [that is, 1/3, 2/3], quarters, and possibly tenths); (b) visual representations of these symbols, perhaps using common objects contained in the classroom or pie charts; and (c) percentage representations thereof, assuming the percentage concept had been introduced. (But certainly no everyday purpose would be discovered to justify performing operations upon them.)

Of course, everyday use isn't the sole criterion for including a topic in the curriculum. Perhaps it isn't even the most important. A topic may never possess any practical utility, but be either (a) a prerequisite for learning a second topic or (b) make the learning of an additional topic considerably easier and therefore consume less instructional time than it would have consumed otherwise. (Criteria such as critical or creative thinking should be avoided since we know next to nothing about how to affect these two constructs. And surely no sane person would suggest that fractional representations could affect either.)

The second genre of questions that curriculum researchers need to ask regarding the wisdom of including a topic in a curriculum falls into that diffuse, difficult, and elusive concept called *transfer*. For any given topic, in way of review, at least three questions should be addressed:

1. *Does topic X serve as an absolute prerequisite for learning topic Y?*
2. *If not, does topic X facilitate the learning of topic Y?*
3. *If "yes" to one of the above, when is the most efficient time to teach topic X?*

Undoubtedly our hypothetical team would conclude that the manipulation of fractions could transfer to algebra and to ratio and proportions (the latter being one of the most useful mathematical/algebraic concepts and the one we are most likely to employ in adult life). But does this lead to a positive response to any of the other three questions above?

To answer them, some additional questions surface, such as:

1. What is likely to happen if operations upon fractions were delayed until the advent of formal algebra instruction?

2. Would this learning deficit impede the learning of algebra? And if so, why not simply teach algebra itself earlier (à la the Fuchs study [Fuchs, Powell, Cirino, et al., 2014] abstracted in this book's companion volume)?
3. Given the availability of all sorts of easy-to-use online calculators (including those specializing in performing operations on fractions), would time be better spent teaching students to use those (if some rationale actually exists for the topic)?

These are the types of questions that curriculum researchers could profitably pursue. Some efficacy researchers might object that this isn't *really* research since it isn't empirical, but in truth it is an integral part of the science of education. And most of these questions can be answered empirically under controlled conditions with a bit of creativity.

ADDITIONS TO THE CURRICULUM

Probably a slightly more difficult (but equally important) area of endeavor for present-day curriculum researchers involves the *addition* of new instructional topics. This is especially difficult within the traditional classroom model for two reasons. First, many teachers will oppose adding anything to the current curriculum because (a) it is easier not to change than to change and (b) they understandably already feel that they are teaching more topics than many of their students can handle.

Of course one option would be to first drop topics and then allocate the amount of instructional time they consumed to new content. Another would be to basically adapt the team-based approach to identifying candidates for deletion to the process of identifying candidates for inclusion.

Thus why couldn't scientists, scholars, entrepreneurs, mathematicians, engineers, economists, writers, public servants, college professors, artists, athletes, and representatives of every arena of endeavor (including employers and employees) be electronically polled to ascertain topics and instructional objectives that they, in retrospect, wish had been included in the official curriculum?

And of course once the technology for preparing a standardized lesson template of, say, thirty-minutes' length becomes available in an extremely simple-to-use format (which would allow written content, quizzes [possibly orally administered via voice recognition], graphic organizers, tables, photographs, videos, sound effects, student choice of talking heads, voice-overs, and other options not yet imagined), then a supplementary curriculum could be generated that might dwarf (but occasionally inform) the official one.

But even if this vision of digital instruction is never realized, surely an important addition to at least the middle school and early high school curriculum would be material supplied by the above professions regarding topics their members believe would:

1. Facilitate entry into their areas of interest (or expertise) for students contemplating a career therein,
2. Give students a feel for what more advanced study is required in the pursuit of related careers, and/or
3. Simply be of interest to students.

What more important topic of study is there for society's youth than to be made aware of the vast number of options available to them and to give them a feel for the types of activities that various careers entail? Who knows what the end-product would look like, but as envisioned here, it would resemble an interactive Wikipedia containing a huge online repository of relatively brief, self-contained digital lessons (some organized as courses) on a staggering variety of topics that could be accessed by anyone, anytime.

BIG CURRICULUM QUESTIONS

A number of curricular questions need to be answered that (*spoiler alert*) are considerably above the present researcher's pay grade, however, these questions should at least be considered by all educational *scientists*, particularly those interested in specializing in curricular issues.

So a few of the more important of these questions will be posed here (but not answered for the above reason) before two major, consummate examples of curriculum research from the past will end our consideration of this crucial component of the educational research process.

Most of these issues derive from the sheer quantity of information available on the Internet (and its 24/7 accessibility within minutes). This gives rise to some very interesting curriculum considerations that researchers (curriculum and otherwise) should be considering. For example:

1. *How important is learning or memorizing discrete facts*? In other words, is it really necessary to know the multiplication facts when everyone has a calculator attached to their smartphone? Is it vital to know who the fortieth president of the United States was? Is there any reason to learn procedures such as one of the long division algorithms?
2. *How important is original learning and its retention*? After all, one can always find an "answer" to almost "anything" at any time on the Internet.

3. *What are the curricular ramifications of this near embarrassment of riches?* Should more emphasis be placed upon critically evaluating such information, or on locating credible information? Will learning itself be considered as important in the future as it has been in the past?
4. *What can be included in the curriculum that can facilitate transfer (which also includes application) of learning?* Can people be taught to be creative or inventive? If so, what should they be taught? Should *understanding* the "*why*" and "*how*" of things be emphasized more than the classic "what, when, and where" "w-h" words? (Note also that 66.7 percent of the letters contained in "why" and "how" contain "w" and "h.")

Questions such as these may seem to belong more to the philosophical realm than to curricular research, but historically they haven't received much philosophical attention and that discipline is presently in even worse shape than education. Also, BIG curricular questions have been addressed in the past, and one of the purposes of including the two curriculum research examples is to illustrate this fact. But first, a prevalent misconception—as prevalent in the past as it is in the present—should be mentioned and awarded the status of our fifth major education urban legend (to complement the four presented in this book's companion volume).

A MAJOR MISCONCEPTION REGARDING CURRICULUM INQUIRY

As mentioned, a huge impediment to curriculum change is its political and socially sensitive nature. However, one educational misconception, if rectifiable, *might* reduce *some* of the impassioned polemics that have always been endemic to the subject. It is a misconception deserving of the status of an ironclad educational principle, which (when positively stated) gives rise to that eagerly anticipated, final education urban legend:

Education Urban Legend #5: Exemplary instruction in some specific subject-matter areas (for example, Latin) or certain challenging skills (for example, the algorithm for "long division" or finding the square root of a number) can:

1. *"Train the mind,"*
2. *Inform the ability to think logically,*
3. *Imbue mental discipline and teach children to work hard,*
4. *Ensure "sensible" voting choices, and/or*
5. *Transfer efficiently to either tangentially related or unrelated subject matter.*

It can't and it doesn't. So, keeping this education urban legend in mind, let's review two of the most innovative curricular movements of the past century, not for historical purposes but rather to illustrate:

1. The repetitive, cyclical nature of the discipline,
2. The relevance of Education Urban Legend #5 and the implications of ignoring it, and
3. The fact that implementing significant curriculum change requires strong leadership and a commitment by multiple individuals and organizations.

CURRICULUM RESEARCH EXAMPLE #1: THE EIGHT-YEAR STUDY

Without question, the "Eight-Year Study" (initiated in 1932) is one of the most ambitious curriculum research studies of all time, and its evaluation (spearheaded by Ralph Tyler, arguably the father of educational evaluation) was certainly the most comprehensive undertaken to that point in time. Professor Tyler was also, if not the inventor of instructional objectives, certainly the most influential early proponent thereof, which assures him a special place in the present author's heart.

The progressive educational movement was a late-nineteenth- and early-twentieth-century reform movement championed by a number of educational philosophers, the most influential and well-known being John Dewey (1859–1952). However the (mostly European) philosophical underpinnings date back a century or more, which many American liberals embraced since they had always been critical of the country's secondary educational process and curriculum.

In those days, the secondary schools were primarily intended (at least according to Wilford Aiken [1942], the chronicler of the experiment) to ensure college acceptance for their students rather than to facilitate their achievement once they were accepted or to have a salutary effect upon their lives afterwards. Progressive educational intellectuals were especially critical of the high school curriculum, believing that it did not prepare students for citizenship in a democracy. (Recall that the 1930s represented an especially turbulent era in US and world history.)

While it is difficult to succinctly summarize the "progressive education" thought generating the curricula adopted in this seminal experiment, Wikipedia probably does the best job of differentiating the approaches and goals between it and traditional educational practice (https://en.wikipedia.org/wiki/

Progressive_education).The more relevant of Wikipedia's progressive characteristics attributed to the Eight-Year Study were:

1. An emphasis upon hands-on projects and experiential learning,
2. An integrated curriculum focused on thematic units,
3. An emphasis on problem solving and critical thinking,
4. Group work with an aim toward developing social skills,
5. Understanding as an important goal of learning rather than memorizing rote facts,
6. Collaborative and cooperative learning projects,
7. Education for social responsibility and democracy,
8. Personalized learning based upon students' personal goals,
9. Selection of subject content based upon future societal needs,
10. An emphasis upon varied learning resources rather than solely textbooks,
11. An emphasis on lifelong learning and social skills, and
12. A de-emphasis on class grades and test scores in favor of students' achievements and accomplishments.

Other strategies implemented by the Eight-Year Study included altering the participating high schools' normal practices via:

1. The use of longer blocks of time than normal class periods,
2. A de-emphasis upon skills that required excessive drill, and
3. Cooperative planning between teachers and students.

In the vernacular, these progressive educators appeared to sincerely believe that a large portion of the secondary curriculum was *worthless*. And while they expressed this sentiment through their proposed curriculum, they would have surely related to the vernacular poetry of another educational philosopher a half-century later:

When I think back
On all the crap I learned in high school
It's a wonder
I can think at all

> (Paul Simon, "Kodachrome," *There Goes Rhymin' Simon*, 1973).

So based upon this background, let's consider the design, implementation, and evaluation of this early, exceedingly impressive curriculum research study as described by the individual most closely associated with it (Aiken, 1942; https://archive.org/details/storyoftheeight009637mbp).

After considerable groundwork coordinated by a committee constituted by the Progressive Education Association (with Wilford Aiken as its chair), the group (composed of well-known and distinguished educators of the time) were reportedly in agreement with the type of curriculum needed to reform American education. The committee members were skeptical, however, that any significant number of secondary schools would volunteer to participate for fear that their graduates would be denied admittance to universities because of the proposed curricular changes that:

1. De-emphasized set unit requirements of instruction in core academic topics and instead concentrated on topics designed to emphasize "the integrity and worth of each individual," and
2. Were based upon the assumption that the optimal development of the uniqueness of each individual is "not only because it is the inherent right of the individual, but also because individual maximum development contributes to the common good." (Ritchie, 1971, p. 485)

But the Progressive Education Association was a prestigious organization in those days at the height of its influence so, with the help of its chairperson, a large number of prestigious colleges and universities were persuaded to relax their admission requirements for thirty secondary schools selected from a larger group who had volunteered to participate.

The schools were allowed to implement the philosophy as they considered appropriate, some inevitably changing their curriculum more than others. In a sense this resembled a scale-up experiment, but this study took place in the 1930s and was state-of-the-art at that time as far as evaluations went.

In total approximately 2,000 students from the thirty schools entered college in September of each year from 1936 to 1939, of which more than half (1,475) were enrolled in thirty colleges in sufficient numbers to justify the intensive interviews that constituted an integral part of the evaluation protocol.

Because the students involved were "higher on aptitude or intelligence tests than the average entering students" of the colleges involved:

> a control or comparison group in each college in which each Thirty School's student [was] matched as exactly as is humanly possible in terms of age, sex, race, aptitude, interests, size and type of home community, and family background. It goes without saying that such a comparison group does not furnish a perfect statistical control, but it is probably as nearly perfect as the measurement of college success in terms of instructors' grades. (p. 148)

[It is interesting that educational researchers were aware, almost a century ago, of the importance of family background variables in determining student achievement.]

The evaluative data sources involved consisted of official college records, lists of honors, examination of students' written work, course test results, and interviews with students, instructors, administrators, and "personnel officers." Today, we might categorize this approach as a sort of "mixed method" evaluation, but there are no modern examples of such studies possessing the comprehensiveness of the Eight-Year Study.

In any event, Aiken reports that "a vast amount of data was accumulated, and the staff gave their summers and most of 1941 to analysis of the collected information." The results were reported as follows:

> In the comparison of the 1,475 matched pairs, the College Follow-up Staff found that the graduates of the Thirty Schools: (1) earned a slightly higher total grade average; (2) earned higher grade averages in all subject fields except foreign language; (3) specialized in the same academic fields as did the comparison students; (4) did not differ from the comparison group in the number of times they were placed on probation; (5) received slightly more academic honors in each year; (6) were more often judged to possess a high degree of intellectual curiosity and drive; (7) were more often judged to be precise, systematic, and objective in their thinking; (8) were more often judged to have developed clear or well-formulated ideas concerning the meaning of education especially in the first two years in college; (9) more often demonstrated a high degree of resourcefulness in meeting new situations; (10) did not differ from the comparison group in ability to plan their time effectively; (11) had about the same problems of adjustment as the comparison group, but approached their solution with greater effectiveness; (12) participated somewhat more frequently, and more often enjoyed appreciative experiences, in the arts; (13) participated more in all organized student groups except religious and "service" activities; (14) earned in each college year a higher percentage of nonacademic honors (officership in organizations, election to managerial societies, athletic insignia, leading roles in dramatic and musical presentations); (15) did not differ from the comparison group in the quality of adjustment to their contemporaries; (16) differed only slightly from the comparison group in the kinds of judgments about their schooling; (17) had a somewhat better orientation toward the choice of a vocation; (18) demonstrated a more active concern for what was going on in the world. (pp. 110–112)

Subgroup analyses were also conducted between those schools that had departed most dramatically from the conventional curriculum and those that had departed the least. The results indicated that the six schools with the greatest fidelity to the experimental curriculum witnessed dramatically better outcomes than the six schools that changed their curriculum the least. (Although perhaps not recognized at the time, subgroup and post hoc analyses should always be interpreted with extreme caution.)

Implications: So did the experimental curriculum actually work? Given the unrepresentative nature of the experimental schools (as defined by unusually high SES of families from which their students came, hence extra instruction they had received) and the weakness of the design (for example, interviewers were not blinded to group membership), we'll never know. But surely this study illustrates the potentially important role that research *could* play in the development of a meaningful curriculum, with the overriding issue always in need of addressing: *What should be taught and when should it be taught?*

So what happened to this curriculum initiative? For anyone conversant with school reform and the history of education, the answer is obvious. Educational reforms come and go, national circumstances change, and styles, philosophies, and fads come into favor and are replaced by others, sometimes to be reintroduced decades later using different terms and vocabularies.

This particular study and its curricular orientation represented the high-water mark of the progressive educational movement, which would soon be rendered untenable by national and world events. One such event was the advent of World War II and the resulting change in the national psyche. And once the war ended, millions of young men returned in dire need of a more "practical" education to help them find work in the job market—thereby influencing the return to a more traditional curriculum.

But this curricular retreat is not how the Eight-Year Study should be remembered. *Its importance lies in reminding us that specific curricular topics that we hold to be completely sacrosanct aren't necessarily prerequisites for future success of any kind.* And perhaps subject-matter instructional objectives don't represent the most important concepts and skills that *can* be taught in our schools. In other words, it was a precursor to the just-introduced Education Urban Legend #5.

After all, the schools' curriculum is designed for more expansive societal purposes than the simple mastery of academic content. And this content must be periodically examined, challenged, and changed based upon national needs—which leads us to the next great national curricular movement—once again precipitated by a national crisis affecting the education of the *grandchildren* of the young men returning from World War II.

This was, of course, the Cold War and it, like World War II, was precipitated by another totalitarian regime. This time around, however, the acquisition of nuclear weapons precipitated a series of events and acts of brinkmanship that somehow failed to mutate into World War III.

CURRICULUM RESEARCH EXAMPLE #2: THE NEW MATH

The impetus for this curricular movement can best be understood by the national setting in which it took place. Today, memories of the constant, low-grade state of crisis and dread of nuclear war with the Soviet Union that permeated American society during the 1950s and early 1960s have been largely forgotten but they were very real in their time. They were, however, buffered to a certain extent by Americans' optimism regarding their self-assured belief in the superiority of their system of government, their military, and their way of life.

If a single event by itself is capable of changing an entire nation's outlook, then the Soviet Union's launching of a small metal sphere into orbit in 1957 constituted just such a phenomenon. Prior to that, not only did Americans consider their way of life and their country's scientific prowess to be superior to the USSR's, they felt the same way about their educational system. So how could a totalitarian regime's schools, whose curricular mainstay seemed to be state propaganda, suddenly outstrip ours? How could their scientists be superior to ours?

Some critics snidely suggested that it was due simply to the Soviet's kidnapped German rocket scientists at the end of World War II being superior to the ones we imported, but that didn't explain why the Germans had such a technological and scientific head start over us.

So it had to be the fact that we weren't *training* sufficient numbers of scientists and/or enough good ones. The answer must therefore lie somewhere within our *schools*. And the most likely culprit was the curriculum. So to the rescue rode not physicists or engineers but *mathematicians* of all people!

In many ways mathematicians would seem an unlikely group to institute a nationwide curricular change. Normally just about any proposed curriculum change engenders impassioned resistance from all sides—the public, educators, and often conservative versus liberal constituencies—but in this case it did not, at least not initially.

One reason for this was that the events just described retrospectively appear to have constituted a near perfect storm. Something besides "business as usual" was obviously needed and mathematicians represented a highly respected profession (as they do today)—although the general public had (and still has) no idea what they did on a day-to-day basis, which was probably a good thing.

Second, as a group they appeared to be completely apolitical, hence they were not suspected of having any agenda other than the national interest. Furthermore, both liberals and conservatives recognized the threat (real or perceived) to national security represented by Soviet scientific advances.

Third, according to Christopher Phillips (2015), the preeminent historian of the new math curriculum initiative, both critics and supporters of the education system of the time, as well as scientists and politicians, had argued throughout the 1950s that the schools' technological instruction was insufficient to produce the number of scientists required to ensure the country's military needs.

And finally, all these disparate groups appeared to be comforted by the fact that mathematicians rather than educators (who seemed to be viewed with even less respect then than now) would spearhead the curriculum changes. Or as summarized more eloquently by Professor Phillips:

> Both supporters and critics of American education found such causes compelling. Longtime educators hailed the emphasis placed on improving schools. Critics of the status quo praised the replacement of educators by scientists as textbook authors. . . . The [New Math] curriculum was born out of the confluence of scientists, educational critics, politicians, and professional educators opportunistically looking to the schools as weapons for the Cold War. (p. 22)

So to shorten the story a bit, a committee was formed, primarily composed of mathematicians, under the leadership of an academic mathematician (Edward Begle), was able to achieve unprecedented funding from the National Science Foundation for the development of a curriculum designed to rectify the situation and, after some expansion, came to be known as the School Mathematics Study Group (SMSG).

The initial concept of the initiative was to concentrate upon the high school curriculum since it appeared to have the most immediate potential to increase the system's output of technological manpower. It was later expanded into the elementary school all the way down to the first grade—an arena in which academic mathematicians in general had little interest.

Rationale and Marketing: The approach the SMSG took in marketing their curriculum change, like the Eight-Year Study before it, was not so much keyed to learning or to the mastering of instructional content as it was to teaching students new ways of *thinking* for both societal and personal benefits. And naturally these expanded ways of thinking reflected the self-perceptions of how the leaders of both movements thought (or believed they thought).

Another commonality between the two studies involved a common goal for all curricular *changes*: preparing students to meet both present and possible future challenges. And in the case of the New Math, the present at least was most definitely fraught with huge challenges.

Mathematics had long been considered the handmaiden of science, especially physics and especially in the late 1950s when computers were in their infancy and occupied an entire room while processing less than the average laptop today. And even desktop electronic calculators (much less handheld devices) didn't exist. Mathematicians (or individuals with prodigious quantitative and calculating skills) were therefore considered essential to bomb and rocket construction.

But while that was one marketing tactic used to sell the New Math, another involved the thinking processes that mathematicians were considered to have developed, presumably as a byproduct of their mathematical education. Mathematical thinking was considered (by mathematicians) to be analytic, logical, orderly, meticulous, and deductive while the progressive movement had stressed more flexible, inferential, and creative mindsets.

And even though the public had no idea what mathematicians do, everyone knew that they must be very intelligent, possessed excellent calculating skills, and were no-nonsense types of individuals unlike most other intellectuals. For their part, mathematicians had absolutely no interest in calculation and, from a curricular perspective, were more interested in teaching students what was (at least to them) the beautifully consistent structure of mathematical systems.

So it wasn't surprising that the SMSG wasn't interested in teaching students how to calculate. Instead they were more concerned with teaching *why* certain arithmetic algorithms worked along with the beautiful, consistent structure of the discipline. And given this knowledge and attitude, they believed that some of these students would go on to have exemplary scientific skills that could be used in the national interest.

Of course most probably also believed (like Latin teachers before them) that the study of their subject matter would train student's minds, inform their ability to think logically in general, imbue mental discipline, and teach the value of hard mental work. But ignorance, or the capitalization on others' ignorance, has always been an important component of marketing.

Products: What set the New Math initiative apart from the Eight-Year Study (and any other curricular movements of which the present author is aware) are the products it developed for its implementation purposes (and the process by which these products were improved).

Given the instructional technology available at the time, the implementation of the New Math curriculum was limited to the two traditional stalwarts available: printed textbooks and teacher workshops. The textbooks emphasized the structure and the why of mathematics and were quite revolutionary at the time, being written with exceeding care by groups of mathematicians and educators during the summer months. They were then introduced to cooperating schools to garner feedback from regular classroom teachers and then revised during the next summer in what appeared to be a thorough and effective, *product development*, quality improvement process.

Demise: The SMSG initiative's shelf life could have probably been extended by a decade or so if the organization had kept to its original purpose of reforming the high school mathematics curriculum. But it did not for several reasons. Some of which were:

1. Parents of elementary school students had been taught almost exclusively based upon memorization, drill, and computation. They therefore had no idea *why* one "borrows" or "carries" in multi-digit computations and probably didn't see the necessity of understanding why. They also didn't understand *why* anyone should bother to learn some of the advocated topics such as performing basic operations in number systems other than the standard base-10 system. And they certainly didn't know how to do it themselves so, consequently, many parents (like their children), couldn't understand the textbook explanations (which often involved sets and seemingly obtuse algorithms that were designed to foster understanding rather than computational efficiency). And this became a problem for parents trying to help their children with homework assignments that they themselves couldn't complete.
2. Elementary school teachers' resistance (partly because many had insufficient knowledge to teach anything besides computation and partly because the SMSG did not possess the capacity to provide large numbers of elementary school teachers with the necessary professional development) eventually doomed the project, and
3. The cyclical nature of education itself where *nothing* is capable of completely solving the discipline's systemic problem of teaching rooms full of children with huge, prior instructional deficits. Thus new, promising strategies—once tried for a time—fail, and someone else who comes up with something else will also wind up failing. And so in the end, the movement atrophied.

However, in its heyday the SMSG's "New Math" initiative may well be this nation's most impressive attempt at curriculum change. Its primary product, mathematics textbooks, were revolutionary compared to traditional textbooks and over the initiative's relatively brief lifespan, the SMSG published, according to its preeminent historian (Phillips, 2015), "almost four million copies of over twenty-six different textbooks." But in the end, like the Eight-Year Study before it, the New Math was replaced by a "back to basics" type of mentality emphasizing something very similar to what it was designed to replace.

So did the New Math work? As with the inability to definitively answer the same question regarding the Eight-Year Study, it is impossible to say categorically. Unlike its predecessor, a single, definitive evaluation was not conducted, although a meta-analysis (Athappilly, Smidchens, and Kofel, 1983) reviewed 134 diverse studies (kindergarten through college) "related to the concepts introduced into mathematics instruction during the 1950s and 1960s." In general, these results were positive, but as discussed previously that is true of almost all educational meta-analyses and this one produced smaller effect sizes than most.

Was the initiative a failure? Again, the answer is destined to disappoint. Certainly the New Math fell into disfavor as did the fate of the progressive curricular initiatives. It should be noted, however, that the SMSG never intended its textbooks to endure and purposefully gave them a brief shelf life by designing them unattractively with soft yellow covers to encourage commercial publishers to replace them with pedagogically equivalent textbooks as quickly as possible.

The commercial publishing houses did just that, often by hiring the authors of the SMSG textbooks with the latter organization's encouragement. And to this day, many of the New Math attempts at fostering *understanding* of the concepts taught live on in modern textbooks.

CONCLUSION

And so the story goes. In some cases curricular change is inevitable and necessary because society's needs change over time. In others, it is endemic to the maddening repetitious nature of education and educational research. Since we know that the curriculum will change over time to meet new societal challenges, real or perceived, it is important that curriculum researchers:

1. Develop an infrastructure to speed the process,
2. Serve as the voice of reason that there is no *curricular content* that will train the mind, persuade people to think logically, teach mental discipline, and so forth,
3. Participate in the creation of curricular products as described earlier, and
4. Evaluate the results of all of these efforts.

Chapter Eight

A Big Science Experiment that *Might* Jumpstart the Science's Infrastructure

Obviously no single experiment in any discipline is capable of assessing the "ultimate limits" of anything, so the clandestine purposes of this proposed study are to:

1. Provide an event capable of capturing the imagination of a public that doesn't even know (or care) that there is such a thing as a science of education and, by so doing
2. Jumpstart the construction of the necessary infrastructure for a sea change in this unappreciated science's trajectory.

In other words, we need to borrow from the similar, somewhat disingenuous but highly successful public relations campaigns launched by physics and medicine to discover the origin of the universe and win the war on cancer, respectively. Except that the initiative proposed here (an abridged version of which was described in Bausell, 2011) has a much better chance of success.

So in a nutshell, the first step would be to secure an inner-city school district's cooperation to allow a rather intense longitudinal study involving pre-kindergarten or kindergarten families to be conducted under its auspices. Near the beginning of the summer, volunteers would be solicited from families whose children were due to enroll in pre-kindergarten classes the following school year. (If these families are too difficult to contact, or if pre-kindergarten isn't available, the study could begin the summer prior to the children's kindergarten year, but henceforth let's assume it begins with pre-kindergarteners.)

There are many, many options for designing this study, one of which is to "simply" randomly assign pre-kindergarteners to two groups, one receiving the intervention and one not. Since this study would be exceedingly expensive, and perhaps would never be repeated, a slightly different approach might be employed to maximize the amount of information obtainable.

The initial goal would be to obtain informed consent from families willing to allow their appropriately aged child to participate, once they understood what was entailed: namely, to have their children tutored for *at least* one full year (summer and school year) and to make them available for testing throughout their entire elementary school experience.

No attempt would be made to generalize the results of the study to parents whose life circumstances didn't permit them to devote the necessary time and effort required to ensure that their children would be available to receive this extra instruction. No dependence would be placed upon teachers' "professional judgment" regarding the extent to which the intervention would be implemented and no time or resources would be involved on the part of the schools except perhaps providing some space after school for tutoring.

The overriding purpose of this study would be to determine what the maximum effect of *massive* doses of additional, relevant instruction time can be. (Obviously this study will fall within the scientific realm of *what could be* since it would be designed to maximize the amount of learning registered by the intervention group as compared to regular school instruction alone—not to demonstrate the practicality of the intervention or how it would later function in a scale-up evaluation.)

COMPROMISES

A number of concessions have been made here to make this already impractical study a bit less so. For example, a second school district serving upper-middle-class families could be employed as a parallel arm of the study since we also have no idea what the ultimate limits of instruction are for this group of children either. Perhaps the *societal* impact thereof might be even more pronounced, but (from an equity perspective) if an "either-or" choice were necessitated, we owe it to the economically and prior instructional disadvantaged students to employ them.

A far more important option, which would make the experiment exponentially more meaningful, would be to add a version of Lynn Fuchs' perspicuous classroom instruction intervention to the supplementary tutoring protocol. This version of classroom instruction, described in experiment #7 (Fuchs, Fuchs, Craddock, et al., 2008) in this book's companion volume, would consist of specifically *trained* and *supervised* teachers *paid* by the study investigators to deliver carefully *prescribed* classroom instruction throughout the school day to intervention students in addition to their supplementary tutoring—either for the entire school day or for several class periods. (Another advantage of this version of the study would be that the same facility could be employed for both classroom and tutoring components of the study—thereby largely eliminating space and traveling difficulties.) This option might also take place in its own space outside of an existing school building and would function similarly to the laboratory schools that were once popular in schools of education.

If society had the *will* to support this latter option, the study purpose would mutate to ascertaining the limits of instruction *period*—at least with respect to the elementary school years. But regardless of whether either, both, or neither of these options are employed, the study's entire modus operandi would consist of packing as much relevant instruction into the time allotted that the students could tolerate. However, for expository purposes let's stick with the extra-school tutoring arm to keep the proposal a bit more practical.

EXPERIMENTAL DESIGN

As part of the screening process for selecting students, a variety of measures would be administered in an attempt to screen out as many children with serious development problems as possible. Not because these children aren't important but because our purpose would be to identify the perhaps 90 percent of children from this population who can benefit maximally from extra instruction and who can ultimately function most productively in society. Another purpose of screening would be to identify families who were able to comply with the experimental protocol, thus it would probably be wise to require all initially volunteered students to come to a fixed number of tutoring sessions prior to randomization in an attempt to predict future compliance.

Since this study would span the entire elementary school experience, the avoidance of attrition would constitute the most serious challenge for the study. Significant logistic problems would also exist with a study of this magnitude, not the least of which would be the necessity of designing a tutoring curriculum and all of its attendant components for the entire elementary school curriculum. Therefore, to provide as much time as possible for this preliminary work (including potentially reducing attrition), a staggered, grade-per-year implementation would be employed rather than a single tutored group versus a single control group.

Thus assuming the study began the summer before pre-kindergarten, volunteered students would be randomly assigned to one of the following eight groups (seven if it proved impractical to recruit pre-kindergarten families), all of whom would have received the same screening protocol. (The constitution of a quasi-experiment group would probably also be wise, consisting of carefully matched students from either the experimental group's schools or similar schools in the same district serving similar families.)

In any case, the very hypothetical design for the randomized portion of the study would be as follows:

Group 1: The children randomly assigned to this group would begin their tutoring experience the summer before pre-kindergarten and would continue to receive the intensive tutoring intervention from then until the end of fifth grade. During the pre-kindergarten year (year 1), the remainder of the sample would proceed with only their regularly scheduled testing activities with all seven groups functioning as a control for group 1. (If the classroom instruction portion of the study were to be implemented, group 1 would receive a structured, individualized beginning curriculum in addition to supplementary instruction while the remainder of the sample received usual preschool activities.)

Group 2: These children would not receive the intervention until the summer before kindergarten, but would receive it from then through the end of the fifth grade. At the end of first grade, they could no longer serve as part of group 1's control, thus groups 3 through 8 would serve as controls for both groups 1 and 2. And so on it would go with the control shrinking one group at a time until only group 8 would remain as the final control for the entire study. (Given attrition, it would probably be wise to randomly assign more students to the later groups than the earlier ones.)

Groups 3–8: Each group would begin the intervention one year later in a staggered fashion. Group 3 would receive the intervention starting in the summer before first grade all the way through the end of grade 5. Group 8 would begin the summer before sixth grade and end at the completion of that school year. (This final year of *tutoring* for group 8 would be irrelevant for the experimental portion of the trial itself since the study would effectively end once all the children were tested at the completion of fifth grade [or at the end of that summer] with the assessment results for group 8 [at both the spring of year 7 and the fall of year 8] serving as the control for group 7 and in a sense for the other six groups as well.)

Of course just because the study had run out of control groups doesn't mean that the students' progress wouldn't continue to be monitored throughout their schooling experience. (If funds could be obtained, it would be preferable if additional supplementary instruction were made available to everyone for as long as they needed it—even if this need extended throughout high school and perhaps college as well.)

However, from an experimental perspective, the experiment per se would be over at the end of fifth grade, although everyone involved with the experiment would have become so attached to these children by this time that no one would want to cut them off from any additional benefits if additional resources could be found for this purpose.

Although a bit unwieldy, the advantage of this design would be that every family who volunteered would be assured that its child received at least one full year of free tutoring. (The average participant would receive a little more than three-and-one-half years of instruction.) This would encourage families to volunteer in the first place, as well as hopefully to remain in the study until its end. Naturally parents would be compensated monetarily commensurate with the study requirements (for example, time and effort required for making students available for testing).

THE CURRICULUM

Although the study might begin with pre-kindergarten children, instruction would always directly involve actual academic subject matter and not learning readiness, developing motor skills, or other pap of such ilk. The initial reading curriculum, therefore would teach the letter names when needed (individual children would never be taught anything they already knew) and then phonics instruction would begin (for example, initial consonants, consonant blends, long and short vowel sounds, and the most common rules governing their expression) along with recognition of as many sight words as deemed necessary (for example, the 100 most commonly found in children's literature), reading brief sentences based upon the child's vocabulary, and comprehension (based upon oral questions following reading).

The mathematics curriculum would be equally straightforward. And as mentioned, the instruction employed would span the entire elementary school curriculum as well as supplementary curricula deemed to be important or tailored to individual children's interests. (As should come as no surprise at this point, instructional objectives would be used to form the basis of this instruction as well as the tests designed to evaluate it.)

ASSESSMENT

Summative tests would be administered to all students (experimental and control) in the study twice per year—once immediately before school began in the fall and once at the end of the year. Curriculum-based measurements would be administered throughout the academic year to the experimental groups (for example, groups 1–4 in year 4).

The summative assessments would be composed of items specifically keyed to the instructional objectives reflecting the curriculum, but for public relations and comparative purposes, the district's standardized achievement tests would also be administered once a year so that the experimental and control groups could be compared to national norms.

INSTRUCTION

The amount of tutoring the participants received would depend upon their attention spans (which would be expected to increase as a function of maturity and exposure to instruction) and their availability, as provided by their families, but as much instruction as anyone would be willing to accept would be provided. Certainly no less than twelve hours of supplementary instruction per week during the school year (which would include weekend sessions) and a full schedule during the summer. And while tutoring would be the primary source of instruction, small group instruction and digital instruction would probably also be employed occasionally. Also, remote tutoring might be used when conditions necessitated it. (If the classroom version of the intervention was to be included, the tutoring schedule would probably need to be lightened a bit.)

Additionally the younger children would be read to for a few minutes following each tutoring session—optimally with their parents or other family members present when possible. An attempt would be made to involve any family members in the process who were interested, such as by providing them with books to read to their children and flash cards to work with them at night or on weekends as appropriate.

Attempts would also be made to persuade the experimental families to limit the amount of television viewing available (or, at the very least, to ensure that what was watched was educational in nature). The latter would be facilitated by supplying each family with a computer upon which only study-related educational materials would be available, such as stories read to the students accompanied by pictures and occasional words for the child to learn. Educational programming delivered by other organizations would be employed as well, selected and made available by study personnel.

The families would be told that the purpose of this experiment was not to remediate their school's instruction but rather to prepare their children to excel academically in order to enable them to reach their full potentials in life. (If this sounds like progressivism, please accept your author's apologies—*this* proposed study would definitely not fit a progressive educator's vision of schooling.) If the classroom option was not implemented (as is being assumed) there might even be a degree of informal counseling necessitated—such as for a child too shy to speak in class, or other areas of concern (for example, the occurrence of in-school bullying that needs to be resolved with the school's help).

HYPOTHESIZED RESULTS

There is little question concerning what the initial results emanating from this design (or some variation thereof) would be. Obviously, the children in group 1 would learn a great deal more during their first year as compared to the children in the other seven groups because, if for no other reason, the children in the control groups would be receiving very little intense academic instruction in preschool and would probably receive little or no extra-school instruction. (If the structured classroom options were implemented, the effect might surpass even the present author's expectations.)

The truly fascinating question, however, is what impact such an intensive and continuing educational intervention would have subsequently. No one knows how much the superiority exhibited at the end of the first summer would increase during the pre-kindergarten year, into kindergarten, during the next summer's instruction, and each year the experiment is continued—only that it *would* increase. (Note that this study differs from early intervention programs whose effects dissipate within the public schools over time in the sense that this one continues to build in potency over the course of elementary schooling in *addition to* the instruction provided by the schools. Or from another perspective, this design would not only assess cumulativeness, it would capitalize on it.)

The major advantage of this design, therefore, would be the definitiveness with which it would answer the following questions:

1. *What is the total effect of children receiving as much extra-school instruction as possible through their entire elementary school experience?* The comparison between group 1 and group 8 at the end of the fifth grade (or possibly the end of that summer) would assess the total effect of tutoring children from the summer before pre-kindergarten through the end of elementary school. The expectations would be that a truly astounding *cumulative* learning difference would accrue between these two groups on all learning and cognitive measures employed in the study.
2. *Is there a point at which extra instruction loses its potential effectiveness (or becomes relatively more effective)?* Our working hypothesis would not predict either outcome, but this question might be definitely answered for the first time because each year a different group begins receiving the

tutoring intervention (one year later than the previous group, hence receiving one year less additional instruction).

Thus, the comparison between group 3 and groups 4–8 at the end of grade 1 assessments would assess the effects of beginning tutoring during the summer prior to grade 1 and throughout the grade 1 school year. The comparison between groups 1 and 2 at the end of kindergarten would assess the effect pre-kindergarten tutoring produced over and above kindergarten tutoring. (If there was very little difference between groups 1 and 2 at the end of kindergarten, the implication might be to increase instructional time in kindergarten or to simply leave pre-kindergarten alone unless a delayed effect occurred—unlikely but conceivable.) And, of course, the comparison between groups 2 and 3 would address the same issue for kindergarten.

3. *What is the relative effectiveness of extra instruction provided during the summer months versus extra tutoring occurring during the school year?* Since students would be tested at both the beginning and end of each school year, it would be possible to assess the differential learning resulting from the intervention during each summer and during each school year for each grade level. These data would also provide a much firmer handle on (a) how much children actually forget during the summer months (since each year's control group would be tested at the end of the school year and at the beginning of the next with no instruction in between), (b) what types of content are more susceptible to forgetting, and (c) how much forgetting summer instruction prevents (plus how much learning it produces since there would always be at least one group that received no summer tutoring). Although highly unlikely, these comparisons would also indicate if summer tutoring was sufficient to end learning disparities (or if school year tutoring alone would be sufficient).

Research of this genre should have been conducted decades ago. And while everyone's grandmother could predict that, say, group 1 (whose participants were tutored throughout their elementary school tenure) would statistically outperform group 8 every year until experiment's end, what no one knows is the *magnitude* of these effects or how rapidly group 1 would close the gap on their upper-middle-class counterparts as assessed by commercial standardized tests.

Of course, no randomized trial ever conducted is immune from criticism. One that might be leveled at this study is that the intervention isn't composed solely of instruction but involves personal contact with caring adults, mentorship, differences in family involvement resulting from participation in the experiment accompanied by support (financial and possibly child rearing education), and a host of other factors. So, even if the results are breathtakingly positive, how would we ever know exactly what produced them?

The answer is threefold. First, the learning results are due to increased instructional time *and* its increased relevance because (according to our working hypothesis) these are the only two factors that improve learning. Second, aren't mentorship and personal contact with adults (including family members) also a form of instruction, broadly defined? And third: *Who cares?*

The purpose of this study is basically to see what it takes to ameliorate the extra-school learning advantages of not being born into an upper-middle-class family. So if anyone ever gets the opportunity to conduct this study, they should realize that there may never be a second chance and they should therefore unapologetically throw everything into their intervention that has the potential of increasing instructional *time* and *relevance*. And this generates yet another question:

WHO SHOULD CONDUCT THE STUDY?

First, this study would obviously be a major undertaking since it might require multiple sites, scores of employees, and several *teams* of researchers. Your author's vote for the principal investigator (or consultant) of the entire project would probably be Lynn Fuchs of Vanderbilt University (assisted of course by Doug) since this team definitely knows how to cleanly conduct large learning experiments and has undoubtedly conducted more of them than anyone (although neither she nor anyone else has any experience with one of this magnitude). She also has considerable experience in training and supervising tutors, constructing tests that match the experimental curricula (or vice versa), and in the development of curricular materials—all of which are integral components of the infrastructure required of this project.

IMPORTANCE OF THE INFRASTRUCTURE CREATED FOR THIS PROJECT

Many of the study's necessary components (for example, space for tutoring, transportation, computer support, staff) are obvious and don't need to be discussed here. Others for which this study would provide an excellent (and perhaps sufficient) impetus for producing have been mentioned earlier and constitute a not-so-hidden agenda for the entire study—namely, to provide a jumpstart for constructing the infrastructure necessary for the proposed science itself, including:

1. The translation of the entire curriculum to instructional objectives accompanied by sample test items for each,
2. Tests based exclusively upon these objectives,
3. And data (lots of data) for the proposed assessment products discussed in chapter 4 (for example, the total number of objectives learned [TOL], the time required for learning them [RLT], and the feasibility of measuring differences in individuals' required learning time [IRLT]).

At some point the study investigators would also identify supplementary topics not included in any traditional curricula since some students will master all of the objectives associated with the latter. How such supplementary topics should be chosen is not clear, but future utility (for example, Internet search procedures, coding, more advanced mathematical content, critical thinking skills) should be one criterion and individual student interests should be another. Perhaps practitioners in the various occupations and professions would volunteer topics they considered important for success in their vocations or to facilitate some other facet of the curriculum mentioned in chapter 7.

However, far and away the most labor intensive and important infrastructural component would be the tutoring protocols and lessons—because this study is not the place to repeat past mistakes, so tutors would not be left alone "do their own thing" or exert their "professional judgments." Every objective in every lesson would have a prepared script for the tutor to cover, which would be on the tutor's computer. (The tutor would not be required to read the script verbatim, but would be required to follow the presented flow of teaching points.)

Also included with each objective would be a sample item or two with which to quiz the tutee during and following instruction—the results of which would be recorded to ascertain what needed to be retaught as well as a means of improving the lesson for future purposes. Each tutoring session would be taped and a sample thereof evaluated to (a) ensure compliance with the instructional protocol, (b) suggest improvements (if necessary) in the tutor's delivery, and (c) for exemplary sessions to serve as training tools for future tutors (as well as to serve as a basis for improving tutoring scripts).

This infrastructure would also be a huge boon for the development of digital instruction by other product development teams. Human and digital tutoring, after all, involve many of the same components and their similarities are much more striking than their differences. Therefore the human tutoring scripts along with the taped sessions would provide a boon for the development of the digital tutoring modules discussed in chapter 2.

Perhaps a subsidiary division of the study could even involve translating the human tutoring scripts into digital instructional modules, for while the vast majority of the instruction would involve human tutoring, it would be irresponsible not to employ digital instruction as well, especially if the classroom version of the study were to be included.

And certainly most forms of testing (for example, the curriculum-based assessments) would be administered, scored, and stored electronically. Also, every test and test item result accruing in the course of a tutoring session (human or digital) would be recorded and quantified for subsequent analysis (perhaps using some version of the Jack Mostow's automated mini-experiments discussed early for quality improvement purposes).

In other words, this study could begin the process of creating much of the infrastructure needed for the migration to a useful and meaningful science of education. Perhaps the study will never be conducted but if it were, it could potentially constitute a steroidal leap forward for the discipline.

Concluding Thoughts

This book's vision of the infrastructure needed for reformulating the science of education is based upon what the author considers to be a very parsimonious and sensible working hypothesis for the discipline itself. Even if this vision is too restrictive for most educational scientists to endorse, perhaps it can spawn superior alternatives, because surely few practicing researchers can be particularly happy about their discipline's current trajectory.

Before concluding, some mention should be made of the funding requirements for such a reformation. When viewing what the science of education's role should be with respect to facilitating the learning needs of all of society's young, what should give everyone pause is the amount of resources currently allocated to hugely expensive projects at the expense of smaller, curriculum-based, instructional ones.

These high costs are unnecessary and inequitable for two reasons:

1. Much of this expense is due to overhead costs charged by the university (in some cases 50 percent or more of the entire budget for federally funded research) and the fact that educational researchers' salaries are enhanced by padded budgets and the inclusion of nonessential personnel. Funding agencies should drastically reduce what they are willing to pay for both purposes and the rate should be reduced inversely proportionate to the overall budget.
2. The expense of efficacy evaluations is due to the large sample sizes required for evaluating interventions that will *obviously* and *tautologically* produce learning when compared to no such interventions if comparison groups are employed that do not rigorously control for instructional time and the experimental curriculum.

There are several potential solutions to these problems, none of which will be received graciously by practicing researchers and all of which will be about as easy to implement as guiding a camel through the eye of a needle. Some of these are to:

1. Reduce the proportion of the educational research budget dedicated to indirect costs (institutional overhead).
2. Give preference to funding smaller, less expensive studies that adhere strictly to the Curriculum → Instruction → Learning ≈ Testing model.
3. Drastically reduce funding to investigator-initiated research topics and instead *prescribe* the type of technologically enhanced products that have the potential to improve the access to, efficiency of, engagement with, and reduction in costs associated with instruction.
4. Abandon the current funding selection process by constituting a panel of research methodologists, Silicon Valley-type entrepreneurs, digital instruction experts, curriculum specialists, and *perhaps* an educational researcher or two charged with (a) operationalizing the direction for the research agenda described above, (b) ensuring adherence thereto in the selection of projects, and (c) prioritizing the funding of infrastructure necessary for the science.
5. Select an educator or education administrator with public relations skills to publicize the change in direction to both garner public support and cooperation from public school districts for testing and implement the instructional and testing products produced.
6. Select a dedicated, persuasive, single-minded CEO-type administrator for the entire initiative such as Edward Begle who oversaw the School Mathematics Study Group or Wilford Aiken who did the same for the Eight-Year Study. This person should be charged with coordinating developmental and funding efforts with the technological community, charitable foundations, the federal government, and civic-minded corporations.

Practicality of these funding suggestions: Certainly none of this can be achieved by the federal government whose track record puts the increment principle to shame. So perhaps a hybrid funding approach could be constituted consisting of a *fund* dedicated solely to the production of instructional *products* (or perhaps preferably to the production of *digital* instructional products) possessing most of the abovementioned administrative and oversight characteristics plus a few new ones:

1. Interested parties (including the federal government, nonprofit foundations, socially conscious entrepreneurs, and so forth) would contribute

directly to this fund but would have no oversight except to ensure that the fund adhered to its previously agreed-upon charter.
2. Either no indirect costs or a minimal, nonnegotiable flat rate (for example, 10 percent) would be allowed.
3. The proposed budget would be vigorously reviewed for nonessential salaries and other padding.
4. No funding would be provided for efficacy evaluations employing business-as-usual (or no-treatment) controls. Limited funding could be available for relatively small-scale evaluations employing classroom instruction, small-group instruction, or video instruction involving identical instructional objectives and instructional time to the experimentally developed instructional product.
5. A portion of the overall budget would be administered *after* the completion of the *product*, which would be evaluated based upon predetermined criteria. (Recall that this fund would be dedicated to the production of something tangibly useful regarding instruction, access to instruction, or increased efficiency thereof—*not* the production of knowledge or interesting relationships or possibly useful adjunctive aids for the creation of future products.)
6. While the resulting products could be marketed for profit, a predetermined percentage off the retail price would be returned to the *fund*.
7. There would be no yearly time requirements for the fund to expend any sizable proportion of its assets in any given year if sufficiently promising proposals were not submitted therein.

Practicality of this book's vision in general: It may well be (in fact it is highly probable) that many of the suggested studies and infrastructure components proposed in this book (for example, the previous digitally enhanced classroom or the "BIG Science" experiment) are far too ambitious to be implemented quickly and must evolve piecemeal over time, if at all.However, if no such evolution occurs at all, then the answers to the originally proposed thought questions in this book's companion volume will be as obvious a *century* from now as they are today. By way of review, the questions were:

> If no educational research had been conducted during this century, would this have deleteriously impacted the American public schools?

Or:

> If no educational research were to be conducted in the future, would anyone but college professors, assorted beltway bandits, and think-tank denizens be any worse off?

The answers to both of these questions will remain the same in the future as they were based upon the evidence presented in this book's companion volume, or in other words: *No*. And that's rather sad, isn't it?

Instead of ending on such a decidedly pessimistic down note, it will be remembered that two different thought questions were proposed for this book, namely:

> *Is it* possible *for educational research to develop into a discipline that* could *constructively impact the education of students?*

And assuming a positive answer to this question, an even more important follow-up thought question was:

> *What type of research would be required (and what infrastructural components would be needed) to do so?*

So the answers to these two questions are how this book will end. The answer to the first question is "*possibly*"; and as for the second, well, this entire book is dedicated to answering that one.

References

Aiken, W. M. (1942). *The story of the eight-year study with conclusions and recommendations.* New York: Harper & Brothers.
Anderson, L. W. (1976). An empirical investigation of individual differences in time to learn. *Journal of Educational Psychology* 68:226–33.
Anderson, L. W., D. R. Krathwohl, P. W. Airasian, et al. (2001). *A taxonomy for learning, teaching, and assessing: A revision of Bloom's taxonomy of educational objectives.* New York: Longman.
Athappilly, K., U. Smidchens, & J.W. Kofel. (1983). A computer-based meta-analysis of the effects of modern mathematics in comparison with traditional mathematics. *Educational Evaluation and Policy Analysis* 5: 485-493.
Bausell, R. B. (2015). *The Design and Conduct of Meaningful Experiments Involving Human Particpants: 25 Scientific Principles.* New York: Oxford University Press.
———. (April 30, 2011). A new measure for classroom quality. *New York Times.* http://www.nytimes.com/2011/05/01/opinion/01bausell.html.
———. (2010). *Too simple to fail: A case for educational change.* New York: Oxford University Press.
Bausell, R. B., and Y. F. Li. (2002). *Power analysis for experimental research: A practical guide for the biological, medical, and social sciences.* Cambridge, UK: Cambridge University Press.
Beck, J. E. (2005). Engagement tracing: Using response times to model student disengagement. In *Artificial intelligence in education: Supporting learning through intelligent and socially informed technology,* ed. C.-K. Looi, G. McCalla, B. Bredeweg, and J. Breuker. Fairfax, VA: IOS Press.
Block, J. H. (1972). Student learning and the setting of mastery performance standards. *Educational Horizons* 50:183–91.
Bloom, B. S. (1974). Time and learning. *American Psychologist* 29:682–88.
Bloom, B. S., M. D. Engelhart, E. J. Furst, W. H. Hill, and D. R. Krathwohl, eds. (1956). *Taxonomy of educational objectives: The classification of educational goals, Handbook I: Cognitive domain.* New York: David McKay.

Bruner, J. (1960). *The process of education*. Cambridge, MA: Harvard University Press.

Cohen, P. A., J. A. Kulik, and C. L. C. Kulik. (1982). Educational outcomes of tutoring: A meta-analysis of findings. *American Educational Research Journal* 19:237–48.

Coleman, J. S., et al. (1966). *Equality of educational opportunity*. Washington, DC: US Department of Health, Education, and Welfare.

Cook, S. B., T. E. Scruggs, M. A. Mastropieri, and G. C. Castro. (1985). Handicapped students as tutors. *Journal of Special Education* 19:483–92.

Cooley, W. W., and G. Leinhardt. (1980). The instructional dimensions study. *Educational Evaluation and Policy Analysis* 2:7–25.

Deno, S. L. (1985). Curriculum-based measurement: The emerging alternative. *Exceptional Children* 52:219–32.

Ehri, L. C., L. G. Dreyer, B. Flugman, and A. Gross. (2007). Reading rescue: An effective tutoring intervention model for language-minority students who are struggling readers in first grade. *American Educational Research Journal* 44:414–48.

Elbaum, B., S. Vaughn, M. T. Hughes, and S. W. Moody. (2000). How effective are one-to-one tutoring programs in reading for elementary students at risk for reading failure? A meta-analysis of the intervention research. *Journal of Educational Psychology* 92:605–19.

Ellson, D. G., P. Harris, and L. Barber. (1968). A field test of programed and directed tutoring. *Reading Research Quarterly* 3:307–67.

Ellson, D. G., L. Barber, T. L. Engle, and L. Kampwerth. (1965). Programed tutoring: A teaching aid and a research tool. *Reading Research Quarterly* 1:77–112.

Fisher, C. W., D. C. Berliner, N. N. Filby, R. Marliave, L. S. Cahen, and M. M. Dishaw. (1980). Teaching behaviors, academic learning time, and student achievement: An overview. In *Time to learn: A review of the beginning teacher evaluation study*, ed. A. Lieberman and C. Denham. Washington, DC: National Institute of Education, Department of Health, Education, and Welfare.

Fuchs, L. S., S. R. Powell, P. T. Cirino, et al. (2014). Does calculation or word-problem instruction provide a stronger route to prealgebraic knowledge? *Journal of Educational Psychology* 106:990–1006.

Gates, A. I. (1917). Recitation as a factor in memorization. *Archives of Psychology* 40. https://archive.org/stream/recitationasfact00gaterich/recitationasfact00gaterich_djvu.txt.

Good, T. L., R. L. Slavings, K. H. Harel, and H. Emerson. (1987). Student passivity: A study of question asking in K–12 classrooms. *Sociology of Education* 60:181–99.

Gould, S. J. (1981). *The mismeasure of man*. New York: W. W. Norton.

Graesser, A. C., and N. K. Person. (1994). Question asking during tutoring. *American Educational Research Journal* 31:104–37.

Hart, B., and T. R. Risley. (1995). *Meaningful differences in the everyday experience of young American children*. Baltimore, MD: Paul H. Brookes.

Hasbrouck, J., and G. A. Tindal. (2006). Oral reading fluency norms: A valuable assessment tool for reading teachers. *The Reading Teacher* 69:636–44.

Kemp, L. C. D. (1955). Environmental and other characteristics determining attainment in primary schools. *British Journal of Educational Psychology* 25:67–77.

Mager, R.F. (1962). *Preparing instructional objectives.* Atlanta, GA: Center for Effective Performance.

Melby-Lervåg, M., T. S. Redick, and C. Hulme. (2016). Working memory training does not improve performance on measures of intelligence or other measures of "far transfer": Evidence from a meta-analytic review. *Perspectives on Psychological Science* 11:512–34.

Moody, W. B., R. B. Bausell, and J. R. Jenkins. (1973). The effect of class size on the learning of mathematics: A parametric study with fourth grade students. *Journal of Research in Mathematics Education* 4:170–76.

Mostow, J., G. Aist, P. Burkhead, A. Corbett, A. Cuneo, S. Eitelman, et al. (2003). Evaluation of an automated reading tutor that listens: Comparison to human tutoring and classroom instruction. *Journal of Educational Computing Research* 29(1): 61–117.

Mostow, J., G. Aist, C. Huang, B. Junker, R. Kennedy, H. Lan, et al. (2008). 4-Month evaluation of a learner-controlled reading tutor that listens. In *The path of speech technologies in computer assisted language learning: From research toward practice*, ed. V. M. Holland and F. P. Fisher, 201–19. New York: Routledge.

Mostow, J., J. Nelson-Taylor, and J. E. Beck. (2013). Computer-guided oral reading versus independent practice: Comparison of sustained silent reading to an automated reading tutor that listens. *Journal of Educational Computing Research* 49(2): 249–76.

Nisbett, R. E. (2009). *Intelligence and how to get it: Why schools and cultures count.* New York: W. W. Norton.

Open Science Collaboration. (2015). Estimating the reproducibility of psychological science. *Science* 349, aac4716:1–7.

Phillips, C. J. (2015). *The new math: A political history.* Chicago: University of Chicago Press.

Popham, W. J. (1971). Performance tests of teaching proficiency: Rationale, development, and validation. *American Educational Research Journal* 8:105–17.

Redick, T. S. (2015). Working memory training and interpreting interactions in intelligence interventions. *Intelligence* 50:14–20.

Ritchie, C. D. (1971). The eight-year study: Can we afford to ignore it? *Educational Leadership* 28:484–86.

Stephens, J. M. (1967). *The process of schooling: A psychological examination.* New York: Holt, Rinehart, and Winston.

Ward, W., R. Cole, E. Bolaños, et al. (2013). My science tutor: A conversational multimedia virtual tutor. *Journal of Educational Psychology* 105:1115–25.

Yeo, S. (2008). Relation between 1-minute CBM reading aloud measure and reading comprehension tests: A multilevel meta-analysis. University of Minnesota, Digital Conservancy. https://conservancy.umn.edu/handle/11299/47844.

Index

Average required learning time, 56–57
Aiken, Wilford, 104
Anderson, Loren, 60

Begle, Edward, 110
Bloom, Benjamin, 54, 60
Bogus assessment principles, 49
Bullying, 69, 121

Classroom instructional products, *see* classroom surveillance
Cumulativeness of research findings, 3
Curriculum research, Additions, rationale fo,r 102; Deleting irrelevances, examples, 97–101; Modern meta-questions regarding, 102–103; Ongoing curriculum review, purpose of, 96; Superordinate curriculum question, 108; Three components, of 95
Curriculum-based measurement for parents, 81–83; Reading fluency research example, 83–84

Decision making in product development research, *see also* Ellson, Choosing between alternatives sans p-values, 42–45; 47–48; P-values, disadvantages in product development research, 39–41;P-values, strategies for increasing, 4–42; Relaxation principle, 44
Deno, Stan, 81
Digital classroom, vision of; Instructional characteristics of, 16–19;Learning technician role in, 17–18
Digital instruction,Infrastructure requirements, 24–28; Research agenda, 30–37; Shared mechanisms with human tutoring, 20–22

Education's BIG Science Study, the limits of instruction, 115–125; Design, 116–119; Infrastructure created, 123–125; Instruction, 120; Outcome variables, 119–120; Rationale 115–116; Research questions addressed, 121–122
Education Urban Legend #5, *see* transfer research principle
Effect size, *see* P-values, disadvantages in product development research

Engagement with instruction, xii–xiii, 31–32, 35–36, 63–64, 70, 79–80; Face-to-face tutoring vs. class room instruction w/r to student questioning, 22–23; Face-to-face tutoring vs. digital instruction, differences, 24; Funding changes required for infrastructure, 127–129; Harris, Phillip, 10–11; Disruptive Behavior; Amelioration In digital classroom setting, 17; Engagement, 63; Early childhood home instruction Hypothetical scenario, 86–87; Infrastructure needed, 88; Lessons from the *Meaningful Differences Study,* 90; Volunteer extra-parental tutoring sources, 91

Eight Year Study as an example of a seminal curricular study; Design and results, 106–107; Lessons learned, 108; Rationale, 104

Ellson, Doug; Contributions to product development approach, 45–48; Programmed tutoring study, 4–9; Evaluation and replication of, 10

Individual required learning time (IRLT), 58–61; Developmental steps, 61; Questions addressed, 61; Rationale, 61

Instructional objectives, 51–56; See also Total Objectives Learned and digital instruction infrastructure

New Math, a second curricular initiative example; Design and products, 110–11; Demise of, 111–112; Historic context, 108–110; School Mathematics Study Group, (SMSG) 110

Progressive curricular philosophy, 105

Remote tutoring, 73–80; Quality improvement, 79; Relationship to digital tutoring, 80; Relationship to face-to-face, 78–79

Research Principles, *see also* bogus assessment principles; Excrement principle, xiv; Grandmother principle, xiv; Prediction of future performance, 50; Intransigence of past learning, 98; Importance of home environment, 89; Strategy for dealing with resistance to change, 98; Transfer, expecting too much of, 103

School Mathematics Study Group (SMSG), *see* New Math

Scope of educational science, xiii

Surveillance, Classroom, 68–72; Questions addressed, 68, 71–72; Rationale, 68

Thought questions informing book; If educational research disappeared, xi, 129; Possibility of a meaningful science, xi, 130

Total objectives learned (TOL), 57

Working hypothesis, xiii

About the Author

R. Barker Bausell, PhD, is a research methodologist, biostatistician, educational researcher, and author of this book's companion volume: *The Science of the Obvious: Education's Repetitive Search for What's Already Known.* He has written twelve other books including *The Design and Conduct of Meaningful Experiments Involving Human Participants*; *Too Simple to Fail: A Case for Educational Change*; and *Snake Oil Science* (all published by Oxford University Press); and *Power Analysis for Experimental Research* (Cambridge University Press). He was the first educational researcher to demonstrate that tutoring could produce significantly more learning than both classroom and small group instruction within a thirty-minute time period when student and teacher differences, time, and the curriculum were rigorously controlled.

He was also the founding editor and editor-in-chief for thirty-three years of the premiere, refereed health evaluation journal (*Evaluation & the Health Professions*) and served as professor and research director in two University of Maryland academic departments during that time period. He has worked with a number of other organizations including serving as (a) the director of the Prevention Research Center of Rodale Press (which publishes *Prevention Magazine*), (b) the methodological and statistical consultant for *Discover Magazine,* (c) a senior scientist for the Delmarva Foundation for Medical Care (which evaluates Medicare and Medicaid programs), and (d) as a research/statistical consultant for several other institutions.

www.ingramcontent.com/pod-product-compliance
Lightning Source LLC
Chambersburg PA
CBHW020747230426
43665CB00009B/528